friendto**friend**series

friend to friend

Enriching Friendships
Through a Shared
Study of Philippians

EDNA ELLISON

New Hope Publishers

Birmingham, Alabama

New Hope Publishers
P. O. Box 12065
Birmingham, AL 35202-2065
www.newhopepubl.com

Library of Congress Cataloging-in-Publication Data

Ellison, Edna.
    Friend to friend : enriching friendships through a shared study of Philippians / by Edna Ellison.
    p. cm.
  ISBN 1-56309-710-9
  1. Bible. N.T. Philippians—Textbooks. 2. Christian women—Religious
life. I. Title.
  BS2705.55 .E44 2002
  227'.6'0071—dc21

                          2001006945

Unless otherwise noted, Scripture quotations are taken from *THE HOLY BIBLE, NEW INTERNATIONAL VERSION®*. Copyright© 1973, 1978, 1984 by International Bible Society. Used by permission of Zondervan Publishing House. All rights reserved.

The "NIV" and "New International Version" trademarks are registered in the United States Patent and Trademark office by International Bible Society. Use of either trademark requires the permission of International Bible Society.

Scripture quotations indicated by CEV are taken from The Contemporary English Version. Copyright© American Bible Society, 1995. Used by permission.

Scripture quotations indicated by NAS are taken from the New American Standard Bible. Copyright© by The Lockman Foundation, 1960, 1962, 1963, 1968, 1971, 1972, 1973, 1975, 1977. Used by permission.

Scripture quotations indicated by THE MESSAGE are taken from *THE MESSAGE*. Copyright© by Eugene H. Peterson, 1993, 1994, 1995. Used by permission of NavPress Publishing Group.

Scripture quotations indicated by WNT are taken from Charles B. Williams, *The New Testament In the Language of the People.* © by Bruce Humphries, 1937; © by Edith S. Williams, renewed 1965, 1966; © by Holman Bible Publishers, 1986. Used by permission.

Scripture quotations indicated by AAT are taken from William F. Beck, *The Holy Bible in the Language of Today, An American Translation.* © by Leader Publishing Co,1976. Used by permission.

Scripture quotations indicated by KJV are taken from *The Holy Bible,* King James Version.

Cover design by Ragont Design. Cover photo © George Simhoni/Masterfile.

ISBN: 1-56309-710-9
N024118 · 0205 · 2m4

Meet the Author

Dr. Edna Ellison has addressed women in almost every state in the U.S. and led women's conferences across Europe and South and Central America. Widowed at an early age, Dr. Ellison earned a living for herself and her children as a high school English teacher, magazine editor, and consultant/director of women's work in several states. She has taught at California Baptist University, Southern Baptist Theological Seminary, Golden Gate Baptist Theological Seminary, New Orleans Baptist Theological Seminary, and the University of Alabama. Her previous books include _Woman to Woman: Preparing Yourself to Mentor_ and _Seeking Wisdom: Preparing Yourself to Be Mentored_ (co-authored with Tricia Scribner). She has two grown children and one granddaughter. Dr. Ellison lives in Union, South Carolina, with her family.

■ ■ ■ Table of Contents

Unit 6: Lord, Help Me See the Truth While I Run This Race

Unit 7: Lord, Help Me Run in This Body Till I Get My New One

Unit 8: Lord, Keep Me on an Even Keel (I Have No Rudder)

Unit 9: Lord, I'm Scared to Be a Leader

Unit 10: Lord, I'm Fruitful and Fragrant. Am I Ready?

■ ■ ■ Introduction

I believe the letter to the Philippians contains the most exciting words of joy in all the Bible. Maybe that's why I love it! It makes my spirit sing! Listen to the joy in your spirit as you study these words. You may enjoy this Bible study with a friend, meeting weekly for ten weeks to discuss the five studies in each unit. The questions in the sidebars are specially designed for you and your friend to consider together, as a way to deepen your spiritual friendship. You may also discuss the unit weekly with a women's Bible study class. Any member can be the facilitator of the discussion as you work through the interactive questions and exercises.

Paul and Silas visited Philippi on their first missionary journey to Macedonia (Acts 16:11–12). As you prepare to explore these thoughts of Paul, don't expect the book to be full of meaningless chatter. Paul knew this letter would be passed around to many churches in Macedonia. He knew these profound words of encouragement would have meaning to others besides the Philippians. He writes them a joyful love letter using a serious tone. He poured out his heart to those whom he loved, to encourage them in hard times.

Paul wrote from prison in Rome, but it wasn't a dungeon. Paul, as a Roman citizen, probably lived in a humble home under house arrest. He might have been chained to a guard and forced to provide his own food, clothes, and other items for survival.

Life was no picnic for the Philippians, either. Almost everyone in town had prejudice against this fledgling "Jewish cult" with these upstart missionaries causing trouble. Yet the Philippian church flourished in its witness and in its love for Paul, who had experienced a great deal of persecution and pain. They all had tasted the sweet joy of Jesus.

Because Paul had a personal relationship with God, he had the characteristics of his Lord: he was a noble leader filled with courage to stand firm. God has much to teach you as you study to enrich your spiritual life.

■ ■ ■

Unit 1:

Lord, Who Am I . . . in You?

■ ■ ■ HAVE YOU EVER WONDERED WHO YOU ARE?

All of us occasionally have an identity crisis. Who you are depends on who God has called you to be. This unit will help you explore your calling from God and the unique way you fit into His purpose for the world.

What do you want to understand when you finish this Bible study? Are you searching for joy overflowing or looking for a fulfilling place in God's plan? This book can help you find those two important treasures: joy and purpose in life, which come only through Jesus. This book will help you find confidence in Him, the Source of all joy and purpose. I pray that as you study this book, you will grow in your knowledge of Truth and establish a personal relationship with Him who frees you from anything that binds you.

If you are studying Philippians with a friend, this unit is an opportunity to find out together who you are. Together you can talk about your experiences and explore the call to community as well as to an individual relationship with Jesus. Ready? Take a deep breath, turn the page, and begin!

Study I

Called as Servant

PHILIPPIANS 1:1

WHEN I WAS ABOUT TEN, I REMEMBER A CLASSMATE NAMED Lizzie who did not show up for school the first day of the fall semester. I asked a friend, "Where's Lizzie?"

"Lizzie got married," she answered.

"What?" I asked. I wondered what kind of father would allow his little girl to drop out of school and live as an adult before she was ready. I knew a lifestyle such as that was not an option for me. That night, as I lay in bed, I felt protected and loved. In my childish way, I thanked God for my daddy and his protection over me.

This unit of Bible study will explore your relationship with your Heavenly Father, whom you may call "Abba," or Daddy. Won't you snuggle up into His arms, where you can feel protected and loved, as you read His words from Paul's letter to the Philippians?

Maybe you are weary of living on your own, and you want to experience the rest found only in Jesus, who says, "'Come to me, all you who are weary and burdened, and I will give you rest. . . . Learn from me, for I am gentle and humble in heart, and you will find rest for your souls'" (Matthew 11:28–29).

As you draw close to Him, He will teach you and lift your burdens. You can learn from His gentle teaching to find rest in Him.

Paul starts the letter to the Philippians with an important salutation: "From Paul and Timothy, servants of Christ Jesus." (Phil. 1:1). From the beginning of this book, Paul sets us straight on a vital principle of Christianity: we are never greater than our Master. If you are a Christian, then you are His servant. Paul always kept his life in proper perspective. He knew he was a servant. He practiced what I call "the art of under-ing," that is, staying under the leadership of Jesus.

- According to Matthew 11:28–29, what does Jesus tell you to do before you learn from Him? *Take your yoke upon you – I will give you rest*

- What does Jesus say He will do? *give us rest*

He is gentle

- What will you find, as you learn from Him? *He is gentle and humble we will find rest for our souls – especially if we are weary and burdened.*

The Art of Under-ing

Paul had learned well the art of under-ing. The process is not easy. It took Paul many years to learn and practice the under-ing principle. Our sinful nature is selfish and greedy. Staying under the authority of Jesus is counter to our natural instincts. Yet we read of spiritual giants, such as Paul—and other Christians over the last two thousand years—who have managed to stay focused on Him. As you study the character of these Christians, you also will find keys to living a life of under-ing. Paul, who wrote these words as a love letter to his dear friends in Philippi, was willing to suffer in prison, to humble himself, and to place himself under the authority of Jesus, come what may. He was willing to be a servant.

Because Daddy Said So

When I was a child, my father had strict rules. He seldom shouted or punished, but he expected his three children to do what we knew was right. He said many times, "Right is right and wrong is wrong, and you know the difference." If we asked why we had to do a certain thing, he would often answer, "Because I said so." (I think most parents, grandparents, or guardians place that rule right up with the Ten Commandments.)

You have a heavenly Father who loves you in an even greater way than any father on earth can. (In fact, if you did not have a very good earthly father, you may have trouble with the concept of a loving father.) When you come under your heavenly Father's authority, He wraps His loving arms around you and protects you. He has given you His Word through passages such as those Paul wrote in his letter to the Philippians, and we obey Him because our Heavenly Daddy Said So.

Like children who feel secure with family rules, you as a child of God can feel secure as you follow His guidelines in the Bible. Because you have free will you can choose to do evil, but as a child of God you can choose to submit to God's rules. In so doing, you find peace, protection, and deep-down joy.

You know the terror and sadness of being shut out from the joy of knowing Jesus, unable to snuggle under His wings. Read aloud Psalm 91:4: "He will cover you with his feathers, and under his wings you will find refuge."

■ Have you ever been outside God's will for your life? Explain. *when I was not close to God - 20-30 years ago. Recently I have grown closer then ever before.*

One of my young friends read Psalm 91:4 aloud this way: "He will cover you with his feathers, and under his wings you will find refuse." I can promise that you will find no refuse—junk or trash—under His wings. Under His wings, you will find promised rest and cleansing. You will be able to lean on the everlasting arms whenever the storms of life bash you. You never need to be outside His will and outside the security of His wings.

Have you ever felt vulnerable, unprotected? Think of those times now. God cares for you, even when you experience bad times. He wants to bring you under His wings to a place of *refuge* (safety) without any *refuse* (trash). Fill in the blanks in the sidebar as you kneel under His wings during this Bible study.

Servant of God's Delight

Though Paul first identifies himself and his young friend Timothy as servants, Paul sees only joy, not slavery, in his servant/master relationship with God. He is a servant of God's delight. He writes to the Philippians a letter overflowing with joy. In the worst conditions in a Roman prison, he speaks of joy again and again.

Zephaniah 3:14 echoes this joy for women: "Sing, O Daughter of Zion; shout aloud, O Israel! Be glad and rejoice with all your heart, O Daughter of Jerusalem." Then Zephaniah 3:17 adds comforting words: "The LORD your God is with you, he is mighty to save." Notice the three things He will do in the next half of verse 17: "He will take great delight in you, he will quiet you with his love, he will rejoice over you with singing."

Imagine a God like that! One who takes great delight in you. Exactly as you are—worthy because God cherishes you. When you are frantic, this verse promises that He quiets you with His love. He rejoices over you with singing!

The Mystery of Transformation: Lifted in Love

Sounds unbelievable, doesn't it? Picture this: you are invited to snuggle under the wing of a Savior who lifts you up and nestles you in safety and comfort against the winds of life. As the servant of His delight, you are changed into a treasured person. Transformed! That is a mystery.

■ Lord, I want to find peace under Your wings. I need peace about: *My Children, my Dad is not a Christian, my brother, Tom.*

■ I want to find safety under Your wings—without any trash. Here's the trash I want to dump:

■ I want to practice under-ing, being under Your care and authority. I now submit:

According to Zeph. 3:17, God will
1. *delight in you*

2. *quiet you*

3. *rejoice over you with singing.*

Study 2

Called to Community

PHILIPPIANS 1:1–2

Begin now to list people who encourage you, especially those who show ethical, moral character.

Anne
Laura
Eileen
Joyce
Dad
Rachel
Sherri

HAVE YOU EVER HAD ONE OF THOSE DAYS IN WHICH A KIND word from one person would have made your day? Yet no one said a kind word, so your day was terrible and rotten. Kind words make a difference.

Before we married, my boyfriend wrote me the most flattering notes. He told me my hair was beautiful, my smile was sweet, and my eyes were adorable. Looking into the mirror, I saw he was right. My hair *was* beautiful. And how about that smile! Then I blinked my eyes about eighty times—they *were* adorable! I hid the letter under my mattress, but almost every hour during the next week I pulled it out to reread those words. What encouragement for a teenager who had never seen herself as so attractive.

Through the years, many friends have sent me letters of encouragement. The letters usually came when I desperately needed them. Paul's letter to the Philippians offers encouragement, but it also serves as a love letter from God straight to you.

In the first two verses of Philippians, Paul says, "To all of God's people who belong to Christ Jesus at Philippi and to all of your church officials and officers. I pray that God our Father and the Lord Jesus Christ will be kind to you and will bless you with peace!" (Phil. 1:1–2 CEV). The NIV and KJV wish the Philippians grace and peace.

From the beginning of this letter, Paul blessed this church with words of encouragement. What these blessings must have meant to them!

Faith and Fellowship, Two by Two

You may be studying this book with a friend. Perhaps you are reading it in a church setting—a Bible study, a Sunday School class, or a mentoring ministry. If so, you may enjoy a close Christian friendship or mentoring relationship. A special friend and confidante can serve as your advocate, guide, servant, teacher, or counselor, and as a sounding board for the ideas you explore. For more information about the roles of a mentor, read *Woman to Woman: Preparing Yourself to Mentor* and *Seeking Wisdom: Preparing Yourself to Be Mentored* by Edna Ellison and Tricia Scribner. You can find both books at www.newhopepubl.com.

Usually the apostles traveled in pairs to support and encourage each other. Timothy was Paul's *merea* ("mah-RAY-ah"), or young friend whom he mentored. Timothy was with him in prison when he wrote the letter to the church at Philippi.

Timothy's family also mentored him. Paul says, "I also remember the genuine faith of your mother Eunice. Your grandmother Lois had the same sort of faith, and I am sure that you have it as well" (2 Tim. 1:5 CEV). No doubt Eunice and Lois shared encouraging words with Timothy as he grew up. As a godly family, they combined faith and fellowship. If you don't have a friend with whom to study Philippians, why not call a friend or family member now, and invite her to study God's word with you? Someone on your list may need encouragement.

Walk Beside Me

You may not have a community of faith. You may wish to pray now, "Lord, I have been out of fellowship with You and with Your people. I want to learn from You and from them. I will find a good Christian fellowship and begin going to church."

You may already be a churchgoer but want a deeper walk. Seek a godly Christian who you know is God's servant, someone in whom you see peace and confidence in the Almighty. Pray now, "Lord, I want to find a Christian friend to encourage me. I will allow myself to learn from her and practice the art of 'under-ing' as a family of God, in community with You."

You may also want to pray this prayer: "Lord, as You take me under Your wing to protect and shield me, I will in turn take someone under my wing. I will show her what You have shown me, nudging her along in her faith, showing her the true sense of community as we deepen our relationship through the years." In an ideal church fellowship, a core group of Christians walk alongside spiritually younger Christians, sharing what they have learned.

Characteristics of the Community

"Community" can mean many things: a neighborhood, an ethnic group, or a cluster of friends with similar characteristics. "Community," as we will use it, describes the closeness of a body of Christians who covenant together in fellowship. As you join them, you should observe two qualities: peace and grace.

■ COMMUNITY OF PEACE Look at the last phrase of Philippians 1:2: "I pray that God . . . will bless you with peace!" The world's peace is fleeting. Friction and greed take over in the secular world and sometimes in the church. Christians learn to forgive one another because we remember how much and how often God has forgiven us. Forgiveness and peace that last always come from God. Isaiah 26:3 says, "Thou wilt keep him in perfect peace, whose mind is stayed on thee" (KJV). Keeping your eyes focused on Jesus brings you peace.

■ COMMUNITY OF GRACE You can receive God's blessing of peace because of one word: grace—and yes, it is amazing! Some call grace "unmerited favor" from God; others call it "kindness." Grace is difficult to define because it is a spiritual process. Ephesians 2:8 teaches, "You were saved by faith in God, who treats us much better than we deserve. This is God's gift to you, and not anything you have done on your own" (CEV). As a child, I memorized this verse this way: "For by grace are ye saved through faith; and that not of yourselves: it is the gift of God" (KJV). "Grace" is God's treatment of us—better treatment than we deserve—through the unmerited favor of a forgiving Lord. Saving grace is the gift of lovingkindness God gives us that ends with eternal life in heaven.

The Mystery of Transformation: Lifted into Lovingkindness

You have been lifted by lovingkindness, or grace. Without deserving it, you have received favor from the God of the universe. Pause for a moment and thank Him for His lovingkindness.

Friend to Friend

Write in your own words what "grace" and "peace" mean:

Grace - God looks the other way when we do wrong. "Unmerited favor" from God

Peace - living with an uncluttered mind. Grieving and depression are gone.

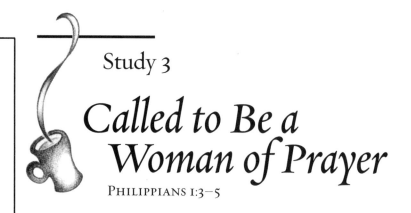

Study 3

Called to Be a Woman of Prayer

PHILIPPIANS 1:3–5

Spend a moment now, remembering your best carefree days of school. List friends for whom you are thankful.

YESTERDAY AS I SORTED OLD PHOTOS, I DISCOVERED SNAPSHOTS of Chrissy and Mary, who are children of a high school classmate of mine, Dollie Meyers. I called Dollie, and after being apart for years, we took up where we left off in our relationship. We joked about old friends and caught up on the latest news about each other. Her town, Sun Valley, Idaho, is a vast distance away—in more ways than one—from Birmingham, Alabama, where I live. We ended our chat with, "As we've said many times, old friends are the best friends."

When I think of the times we had, I am thankful for Dollie and other friends I grew up with: Mary Keith, Dawn, Margaret Ann, Elaine, Florence, Emily, Sara, Jackie, and many others. How about you?

Thanks for the Memories

Every time I get in touch with Dollie, I promise to write, but I seldom do it. Yet in spite of restrictions on his freedom and slow mail delivery in his day, Paul wrote to the Philippians, saying, "I thank my God every time I remember you" (Phil 1:3). To whom do you need to write this week, thanking them for what they have meant to you? As a part of this study time today, get paper and pen, and write.

For what other things are you thankful? *my family, my friends, my dog*

The heart of a woman of prayer is filled with thankfulness and a need to communicate with her Creator. Listen carefully to God. He eagerly calls you to prayer. He desires to bring you into His presence. Take that first step. Ask Him to teach you more about prayer. "'Lord, teach us to pray'" (Luke 11:1). Check the boxes below that apply to you:

Friend to Friend

☐ Lord, I want to be a woman of prayer.
☐ The truth is, I don't have time to pray.
☐ I want to know more about God's word, not about prayer.
☐ Maybe I am called to a community of Christians to pray with them.
☐ I believe God is calling me to be a woman of prayer.
☐ I'll have to think about this for a while.

One of my best mentors once told me, "I pray when the sink is filled with dirty dishes. That's when I need to be most thankful."

Another godly woman told me, "I start a prayer before I get out of bed each morning, and I pray almost every moment all day long. God goes with me and speaks to me as I listen."

As a reminder, you might place Scriptures about prayer around your house or other workplace. Becoming a prayer practitioner takes time. Practice it this week. _Luke 11:1_

If you have children, you could start a Thanks Notebook in your family, adding daily to your list of friends and things you are thankful for. I found the following sentence in an old spiral notebook from years ago: "I'm thankful for old friends, daffodils in spring, sunshine on a cold day, and a microwave oven." Today, for starters, I might add to the list two children, two children-in-law, and one grandchild. It takes only a few minutes, but what a treasure a Thanks Notebook would be for your children and grandchildren (or nieces, nephews, and neighbors' children), to show them you thank God for every memory of them.

When is a good time for you to pray?

Dealing with the Memories

Some memories are more difficult to deal with than others. You may be dealing with memories that bring no joy to your heart. Ask God to help you forgive the people who hurt you, and then mentally place these hurtful memories into a corner of your heart where you can forget them. Like old dresses in the attic, place these memories away, so cobwebs will cover them. Then close the door. Don't dabble in the cobwebs. If you need further help, seek it through a twelve-step program or counseling to make peace with your past. Now is the time to deal with those memories, good or bad. Begin by talking about them with a friend, pastor, counselor, or mentor.

Joyful Requests

Paul says, "In all my prayers for all of you, I always pray with joy because of your partnership in the gospel from the first day until now" (Phil. 1:4–5). Oh my friend, as you read these words, do you find joy in thinking of the Christian partners you've known through the years? Do you smile when they come to mind? No joy is greater than remembering Christian friends or mentors who helped you through the rough spots. Now that is true joy, which goes beyond outer happiness.

Prayers Together

How many times in Philippians 1:4–5 do you find the word "all"?

"In all my prayers" indicates that Paul prayed for the Philippians often. He often prayed for *all* of them. How about you? Do you have a set time and place to pray daily? I realized one day that I'd always be distant from God until I got to know Him better. I determined to make an appointment to meet Him every day. In my hurried life, I've not always been faithful, but I find it's easier to pray daily if I set aside the time as a habit. (Forming a habit requires about three weeks.) I find time in late afternoon—just after work—to relax and enjoy Him. When my children were small, their naptime was my prayer time. God understood when I dozed off in the middle of "Dear God . . ."

When visiting a family in Ireland, I sat at the table waiting for them to "return thanks." Instead, they grabbed the food, even forgetting to pass me some of the items. What a shock! No prayer before meals left me feeling homesick. I missed my church and my family, who prayed before every meal. For me, prayer with others is important. I gain strength from group prayer and from hearing my name and theirs lifted up to our Lord. Philippians 1:4 reads, "Whenever I mention you in my prayers, it makes me happy" (CEV). Like Paul, I am happy when I mention a good friend or when I hear her mention me in prayer. In addition, breakthroughs of the gospel occur when I faithfully intercede for people and for

Spend time with your study partner praying for each other. Thank God for giving you this unique friendship!

situations. I don't know how God does it, but He gives us power beyond ourselves when we join Him in intercession—and He changes us in the process.

The Mystery of Transformation: To Him Be the Glory

Paul says, "Now to him who is able to do immeasurably more than all we ask or imagine, according to his power that is at work within us, to him be glory in the church and in Christ Jesus throughout all generations, for ever and ever! Amen" (Eph. 3:20–21). Through prayer we can transcend time and space. The power of our prayers makes a difference in the world. Yet this is the greatest mystery: God transforms *us* as we pray. To Him be the glory forever and ever!

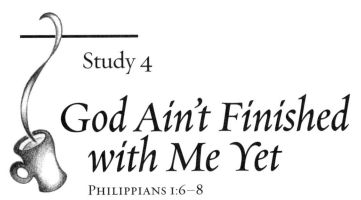

Study 4

God Ain't Finished with Me Yet

PHILIPPIANS 1:6–8

WHEN MY HUSBAND DIED IN 1980, I THOUGHT I MIGHT AS WELL DIE, too. After all, I reasoned, I didn't know how to do anything. I couldn't balance my checkbook accurately, I was a weak disciplinarian for the children, and I never did learn how to keep a spotless house. The first time I cut the shrubbery with the electric hedge clippers, I cut the cord in two—fire shot out in every direction! I couldn't drive the old stick-shift truck my husband left in the driveway, especially when the transmission slipped and someone had to lie under the cab in the middle of the intersection where it stalled and hammer the gears back into place. As long as I had my husband to help with these things, I had confidence. After he died, I didn't think I could stand up to the task of rearing two teenagers, making a living for them, and paying for their education.

Friend to Friend

Think right now of a "dare prayer." *Lord, believing you can do something about the worst situations, I dare to pray for:*

A Woman of Confidence

I am a different woman today. My children are in their thirties, successfully working at good jobs. (What a surprise that they did not become juvenile delinquents!) God picked me up and carried me many of those days in the '80s. A friend invited me to go to a writers conference with her and I said no, because I had no money. I later found an envelope at home, containing the exact amount for the conference tuition. I went with her and have since written five books and hundreds of Christian magazine articles. I became an editor of *Royal Service*, the flagship magazine of Woman's Missionary Union, the largest Protestant women's organization in the world—and I can't claim credit for the job. I didn't apply for it; I didn't even know they were looking for an editor! After my children started college, God picked me up and placed me in this new area of service.

Later I moved to Fresno, California, across the continent from my family in South Carolina. I was confident I could make it on my own. In 1980, I had never flown in an airplane; today I fly all over the world as a ministry consultant and conference speaker. I've spoken to large crowds at women's events in Frankfurt, Germany; London, England; and several Latin American countries, besides many states in the US. Is this the scared young woman who leaned on someone in whatever she did? Yes, I found out the secret to confidence: leaning on God.

Paul declares his confidence in verse 6: "Being confident of this, that he who began a good work in you will carry it on to completion until the day of Christ Jesus." Like Paul, you can be a confident Christian. You can grow in your view of who you are in Christ, who fulfills His purpose in you.

A Jesus Woman

A woman known as "The Jesus Woman" moved to my hometown, Clinton, South Carolina, in the sixties. "Is she a preacher or evangelist in your denomination?" I asked one of her church members.

"No," he said, "she's just a Jesus woman." He paused. "You know what that verse says in the New Testament? 'He who began a good work in you will carry it out and complete it until the day Jesus comes' (Phil. 1:6). All of us can see the Lord completing her day by day among us."

I often thought about what that man said. God had begun a good work in the Jesus Woman, who reflected her Lord, and He would one day complete it. I asked God to let me reflect Him, as a confident Jesus woman, not ashamed of Him in my everyday life and complete one day in Him.

God started a work in you a long time ago. Genesis 1 says, "God saw that the light was good, and he separated the light from the darkness. . . . So God created man in his own image, . . . male and female he created them. . . . God saw all that he had made, and it was very good" (Genesis 1:4, 27, 31). God made you; He created you for a reason, and all that He made was very good. He created you to be a person of goodness with purpose in life.

A Piece of Work

Not only did God create you but also planned in advance the work for you to do. "For we are God's workmanship, created in Christ Jesus to do good works, which God prepared in advance for us to do" (Eph. 2:10). As the Philippians helped Paul in prison, you can help suffering people, or, like Paul, you can share God's good news.

If you can help children finger paint, He may be calling you to do the church bulletin boards. If you have a flair for words, He may be calling you to write a poem for the church newsletter, design or edit the newsletter, or start one if your church doesn't have one. If you like singing in the shower, you may be the church's next praise team soloist.

Paul says, "You have a special place in my heart. So it is only natural for me to feel the way I do. All of you have helped in the work that God has given me, as I defend the good news and tell about it here in jail" (Phil. 1:7 CEV). Stated another way, Paul says, "All of you share in God's grace with me" (NIV). What a joy to share in God's grace! What an identity you have as a servant, reflecting your Master in all you do!

A Work Performed on Stage

Notice where Paul was when he defended the good news: in jail. You might imagine a great courtroom for his defense. Picture a giant stage with a spotlight shining on the star, the well-educated, Jewish Roman citizen, Paul, who could speak with such wisdom. No, God did not plan it that way. Paul, formerly Saul of Tarsus, sat

Friend to Friend

What do you believe God is calling you to do?

What part of your identity may God use in an unbelievable way?

in jail, waiting for his execution. It may sound like a place of despair, but it was a place of brightness and light. God transforms all our stages: a mother stands beside the crib of a child in the sunlight; a sister stands beside her brother and sister who are acquitted of murder; a grandmother touches a newborn granddaughter; a single woman touches the shining cheek of an orphan whom she can comfort. All of these are places of brightness.

Paul and his fellow Christian prisoners sang in jail, just as you and I can sing as God gives us an identity with Him.

The Mystery of Transformation: Darkness into Light

Thank God for the mystery of these words from 1 Peter 2:9: "You are a chosen people . . . belonging to God, that you may declare the praises of him who called you out of darkness into his wonderful light." As you move toward the shining face of Jesus, He transforms you to shed light in the darkness around you. God has chosen you and stamped you with His identity, almost as if His initials are shining forth from you. "'I will make you like my signet ring, for I have chosen you, declares the LORD Almighty'" (Haggai 2:23). Step out of the darkness, O confident Jesus woman!

Study 5

The Whole Is More Than the Sum of Its Parts

PHILIPPIANS 1:9–18

LAST WEEK MY FRIEND AND I TALKED ABOUT HER BROTHER who had moved away. "You know," she said, "I don't understand why so many people loved him so."

I nodded and said, "They continue to remember him and mention him to me often, too, now that he's out of town."

She said, "He is just an ordinary guy. Not particularly handsome, wealthy, or articulate."

"No," I said, "He is extraordinary. He is a godly man, the way he served as a deacon, a servant at church. He tries his best to live a godly life." We decided that his height was average, his nose was nothing special, and his eyes were ordinary, but God had done something special in him—just as He does in all of us. When Jesus enters our hearts, suddenly we are greater than the sum of our parts.

Counted in Love

Take a look at Philippians 1:9: "I pray that your love will keep on growing" (CEV). I've read that when a husband dies, his wife usually remembers him as bigger than life. She may have nagged him or even cursed at him in life but only praises him after he's gone. She remembers few arguments. Sometimes we hardly notice someone in life, yet we grow in our love for that person after he or she is gone. You see this phenomenon when famous people die, such as James Dean, Marilyn Monroe, and Elvis. Once they are gone, they seem bigger than life. (Now if you are an Elvis fan, don't write me a poison-pen letter!)

Paul urges the church members at Philippi to grow in their love for each other. Do you inflate your ego as you look honestly at your capacity to love others? Do you love others unselfishly? My pastor once listed the three love relationships: love God, love yourself, and love others. These three dimensions of our love are essential. Loving God helps you to love yourself. Loving yourself gives you the capacity to love others. Love grows when it's well balanced. The whole of our love is more than the sum of its parts.

Counted in Excellence

Let's look at the last half of Philippians 1:9 (CEV), followed by verse 10: "And that you will fully know and understand how to make the right choices. Then you will still be pure and innocent when Christ returns." Although none of us is totally innocent, we can learn to make wise choices to keep ourselves pure.

Great! I make wise choices. I have a perfect life, right? No, making wise choices is not related to *what* you do but *who* is working within you. When you choose to let the living Lord dwell in you, you become purer and more than the sum of your parts.

Friend to Friend

Check off each of these characteristics of love in which you excel (from 1 Corinthians 13:4–8):

Love is
patient ☐
kind ☐

Love does *not*
envy ☐
boast ☐

Love is *not*
proud ☐
rude ☐
self-seeking ☐
easily angered ☐

Love does *not*
keep a record of wrongs ☐
delight in evil ☐

Love
rejoices with the truth ☐

Love *always*
protects ☐
trusts ☐
hopes ☐
perseveres ☐

Love never fails ☐

What are you willing to give up for God's sake? (Check all that apply):

- ☐ Gossiping with my neighbors
- ☐ Smoking
- ☐ Drugs
- ☐ Unfaithfulness to my spouse
- ☐ Eating too much
- ☐ Un-edifying television shows/ novels
- ☐ Screaming at my husband or children
- ☐ Going to ungodly clubs
- ☐ Looking at pornography
- ☐ Buy less
- ☐ Watch T.V less
- ☐

In his letter to the Corinthians, Paul says love is "the most excellent way" (1 Cor. 12:31). God is counting on you to live in love. When you love God, you put off the old and put on the new. You ask Him to renew your mind with His love so you can love others.

In what ways do you live contrary to who you are in Christ?

Paul says, "Live by the Spirit, and you will not gratify the desires of the sinful nature. For the sinful nature desires what is contrary to the Spirit" (Galatians 5:16–17).

Ask God what He wants you to do. Your issue may not be listed in the paragraphs above. Write in the margin one way you will choose to change your life to a more excellent way.

Meanwhile, Paul says, "Jesus Christ will keep you busy doing good deeds that bring glory and praise to God" (Phil. 1:11 CEV). If you're like me, you don't want Christ to keep you any busier! However, when Jesus Christ comes into your life, He will alter your priorities, so you will find time to do good deeds. When you erase ineffective activities in your life, you will find creative ones from God. In them you will find a solid Christian identity. You will know who you are and whose you are.

Filled with Purpose

Instead of wallowing in his despair, Paul sees purpose in his time in jail. "What has happened to me has really served to advance the gospel. As a result, it has become clear throughout the whole palace guard and to everyone else that I am in chains for Christ" (Phil. 1:12–13). Imagine what an influence Paul had, even with Caesar's staff! Who would have believed it!

Paul sees this renewed sense of purpose in others also. "Most of the brothers in the Lord have been encouraged to speak the word of God more courageously and fearlessly" (Phil. 1:14). In Christ, a sense of community that gives you Christian identity can also nudge you to a more excellent way.

Filled with Joy

Paul goes on to mention others who preach about Christ, some sincerely and others out of selfish ambition, just to stir up trouble (Phil. 1:15–17). He says, "But what does it matter? The important thing is that in every way, whether from false motives or true, Christ is preached. And because of this I rejoice" (Phil. 1:18).

If you knew a Christian was selfishly stirring up trouble for another Christian, could you say, "What does it matter?" as Paul did?

☐ Yes   ☐ No

Why or why not?

What would you say to Paul in such a case? ⤙

If Paul could speak to you today, he might ask you, "Having trouble? Keep on smiling. Sad things happening? Grin a lot. Problems? Keep your eyes on Jesus. Focus on Him and no one else. If Christ is preached, be happy. Because of this I rejoice. Even in prison I smile a lot. I sing. I pray. I praise God! 'Yes, and I will continue to rejoice' (Phil. 1:18)."

Pray silently a moment now.

The Mystery of Transformation: All Things Work Together

Paul says in Romans 8:28, "And we know that in all things God works for the good of those who love him, who have been called according to his purpose." Here is the mystery of this verse: God transforms even bad things to work for good in our lives. Our happiness does not depend on outer circumstances.

As God touches you, He transforms your heart into His heart, your disaster into blessing. In such a miracle, God changes you: once you are whole, you become more than the sum of your individual parts.

How easy would it be for you to forgive a pastor who had preached in your church with bad motives?

How have you been hurt from such a situation?

Unit 2:

Lord, I'm Walking Through an In-and-Out Life

■ ■ ■ A FEW YEARS AGO WHEN I TAUGHT HIGH SCHOOL senior English, I stopped a fight between two students. "Why were you fighting?" I asked.

"He stole my walk!" said one student.

"I did not! He stole *my* walk," said the other.

Both demonstrated their walks. One swayed with his arms hanging low; the other swaggered as he slid across the floor. We settled the matter, but I chuckled about how their ways of walking marked their individuality. Then I walked down the hall with *my* walk!

Once Christians know who they are, they begin to walk in a new life of confidence. Paul begins Philippians 1:20 with an interesting idea: "I eagerly expect and hope that I will in no way be ashamed."

In the next five studies, examine the way you walk through life. Compare your Christian walk to Paul's. Find out how you, like Paul, can walk from shame to boldness, from fear to courage, from sadness to joy, from hatred to overflowing love. Take a long, hard look at how you walk alongside Christians and non-Christians. Ready? Okay, turn the page!

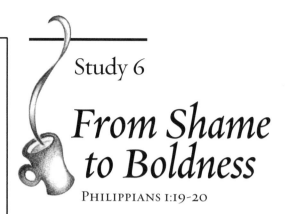

Study 6

From Shame to Boldness

PHILIPPIANS 1:19-20

MANY OF US GREW UP WITH CONFIDENCE BECAUSE WE HAD Christian parents who encouraged us to be the best we could be. In that same family tradition, I expected the best from my children. After they became Christians, their heavenly Father expected the best from them.

Recently I boarded a plane for Phoenix. "You idiot!" I heard a man behind me say. "Don't do that, you idiot!" And later, "Here comes the flight attendant. Will you settle down, you idiot! Don't fidget with your seat belt." I heard him say "idiot" many times in the next few minutes, so I finally turned around to see what kind of man would speak to his child with such disrespect. What a surprise to discover that the man was speaking to his wife! Can you imagine how she felt? I felt sorry for her, yet I wondered why she did not protest. My guess is that she had been beaten down for so many years that she believed she deserved such verbal abuse. I'm sad when I think of her. I pray that God will help her walk in peace and dignity.

Expectations and Hope

Like the woman on the plane, you may have worn a "shame badge" for so long that it feels comfortable. However, nothing anyone did could cause Paul to feel shame. He says, "For I know that through your prayers and the help given by the Spirit of Jesus Christ, what has happened to me will turn out for my deliverance. I eagerly expect and hope that I will in no way be ashamed, but will have sufficient courage so that now as always Christ will be exalted in my body, whether by life or by death" (Phil. 1:19–20).

Staggering Along

Sometimes you may walk with a limp because of abuse. The abuse does not have to come from someone else—a jealous boyfriend or husband, a parent, or a child—it may come from you. When you drop something on the floor (such as purple grape juice on the cream-colored carpet), do you use abusive self-talk? For example, "Oh, Edna, why did you do that? Because you are a dummy, I guess." Or have you ever said, "Just my luck! As usual, I'm a loser." Or "No matter which checkout line I go to, it's always the longest." Even Christians can fall into the bad self-talk habit. We sometimes shame ourselves automatically.

Practice complimentary self-talk this week. Also, put a star in the margin beside any of the following three descriptions that apply to you:

1. TIRED TO THE BONE

I don't use bad self-talk, but I live in survival mode. I'm physically, emotionally, and spiritually tired. I'm burned out. (Check your daily schedule now, and consider if you are burning yourself out with too many jobs, responsibilities at church, or a "Superwoman" lifestyle.)

2. TREKKING ALONE

Sometimes I feel as if I'm going "where no man has gone before." I'm afraid to think I need help, much less to ask for it. (John 16:32 says, "I am not alone, for my Father is with me." If you want someone to walk beside you, ask in Jesus' name, who said, according to John 16:23, "I tell you the truth, my Father will give you whatever you ask in my name." He will walk beside you all the way. If you want a friend or mentor, ask Him for one, and He will send one. He has given you His word.)

3. SOARING IN MY ZONE

I don't need help from anyone. I'm doing okay, walking by myself. I like being independent. I have no problems, and I'm in tiptop condition in every way. Everybody loves me. I smile all the time, and I never cry. (Are you real? You may have problems with reality. Talk to a friend.)

Friend to Friend

This week, practice saying good things to yourself. Which of the following can you honestly say to yourself?

- ☐ "Jesus has made me worthy."
- ☐ "You handled that intelligently, Ms. Brain!"
- ☐ "I know I'm good because of God."
- ☐ "You are great! Next you may be Empress of the World."
- ☐ "You're looking good today!"
- ☐ Other:

Not long ago I told some funny stories at a women's meeting in my church. One woman in my Bible study class later said, "Oh, Edna, you were in your element!" Storytelling is "my element." I love telling funny stories. You probably have a talent or a comfort zone where you seem to be in your element. What confidence you can have as you walk in the zone God has prepared for you!

When I was in the eleventh grade, I memorized these lines from the poem "To a Waterfowl" by William Cullen Bryant:

"He who, from zone to zone,
Guides through the boundless sky thy certain flight,
In the long way that I must tread alone,
Will lead my steps aright."
(29–32)

Years later I was traveling east of Atlanta, Georgia, when I heard tornado warnings on the radio. It was raining hard when I heard, "and the tornado is moving east of Atlanta on I-85." Yipes! I was on I-85! I uneasily looked into the black sky as the windshield wipers worked hard to swipe the pouring rain. I reached the South Carolina border, relieved, when I heard, "The tornado has just passed into South Carolina and is near Anderson." I had just passed the exit for Anderson. Again I searched the skies. When I looked up, I suddenly remembered that poem of long ago and the leech gatherer in the poem who wandered in a wetland. As he looked up from his work to see a soaring waterfowl (a duck or a crane, I suppose), he knew the God who guided that fowl through the boundless sky would also lead his steps in the right direction.

As I drove along I-85, I relaxed. I quit searching the skies. I knew the God of the universe was in control. I did not have to live in fear. I could hope with great expectation.

Countering the Enemy

Look back at Philippians 1:19. What two things did Paul rely on for help in time of trouble?

1.

2.

List three people you can count on in troubled times:

Based on this verse, how do you know he had hope in the future?

Paul had confidence and a steadfast faith in Jesus Christ. These countered his enemies, whoever they were! Prison bars did not confine his hope.

Walking Inside My Body

Regardless of where you walk, you are confined inside your body. Look at verse 20: "I eagerly expect and hope that I will in no way be ashamed, but will have sufficient courage so that now as always Christ will be exalted in my body" (Phil. 1:20). Like Paul, you can pray that God will give you courage to walk without fear, to exalt (lift up and honor) your Lord in the way you walk and in the places you walk. Paul's main concern was that he would not cause shame to the name of Christ, that he would live or die with hope.

The Mystery of Transformation

In 2 Corinthians 12:9-10, Paul writes, "But he said to me, 'My grace is sufficient for you, for my power is made perfect in weakness.' . . . For when I am weak, then I am strong." Whatever your weakness, God can make that your crowning strength. He can change your walk before others into a confident strut, as He fills you with strength and power.

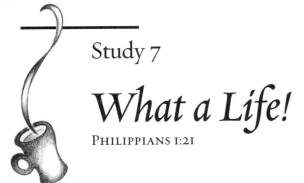

Study 7

What a Life!

PHILIPPIANS 1:21

WE ENDED STUDY 6 WITH A PARADOX: GOD'S STRENGTH IS magnified in a Christian's weakness. How could that be? It makes no sense in an ordinary world, but it is a magnificent truth in the spiritual world, where God reigns.

How is God's strength made perfect in your weakness?

I can call on him to help me I can call on him when I feel alone to comfort me.

my chaos — God can help me correct.

What are some of your common self-talk phrases?

I am a cheerful person
I am learning God's Way
I can do it w/ God's help (anything)
It will all turn out

What are some ways you could talk yourself into God's aims?

When something awful happens let God handle it. Pray.

About a year ago, I was preparing a speech for a women's retreat. I wrote voluminous notes and printed my outline in large letters, so I could read the notes without my reading glasses. I designed a few handouts with flowered borders, copied them, and then relaxed, knowing everything was ready. I left the house in plenty of time, arrived at the airport, and boarded the plane. Relaxing after takeoff, I opened my briefcase to review my notes. The pouch was completely empty. In my mind's eye, I saw all my teaching materials neatly folded on my desk at home, ready to go.

At times like that day, I struggle to use affirming self-talk. I decided that day on the plane that when I get to heaven, I'll ask God why He did not make our brain cells connect but instead created that junction called a "synapse," in which impulses have to jump across to the next nerve cell so you can think or remember.

Synapses or no synapses, I felt pretty stupid that day on the plane. I could choose to either fret my way through this or pray through it. I prayed, "Dear Lord, I am claiming Your Word today—that Your strength is magnified in my weakness. O, Lord, I am so weak! Please give me something to say today. Show me how to teach without any handouts and notes. I am totally dependent on You." I began to listen to His still, small voice (1 Kings 19:11–12 KJV), and He showed me some unbelievable things.

Later at the conference, we did several creative activities; people enjoyed themselves and interacted in ways I had never facilitated before. During the closing session's commitment time, a woman invited Jesus to be her Savior! Her friends gathered around her, smiling and weeping. To my amazement they said, "For weeks we have prayed the speaker would do something like this to share the way to salvation. In fact, we prayed you'd say the exact words you said this afternoon. How did you know?"

I didn't. God did. He always knows, and He is always strongest when we are weakest. I have learned to step back, not to plan so hard and so logically, and to listen to Him before I open my mouth . . . well, most of the time.

To Live Is Christ

The first half of Philippians 1:21 says, "For to me, to live is Christ." Paul's words fit the paradox above. As I diminish my life and my self-importance, Christ becomes more prominent. His strength is magnified in my weakness. I live in Him and for Him. If the above paradox is not enough, Paul presses his point further: "and to die is gain" (Phil. 1:21). At first glance, my logical brain says, "How could this be true? It is never advantageous (gain) to die. For goodness sake, that's the worst thing that can happen."

Let's take a closer look at both halves of this verse.

You can look at Philippians 1:21 in two ways: First, to live is Christ. In other words, your very life is wrapped up in Christ. Jesus is all. He is worth dying for. If you are alive, you will be living for Christ. After all, He died for you and gave you life—eternal life in heaven as well as triumphant life on earth. You live well every day, with hope and joy, because you know Him. As the song says, "life is worth the living just because He lives."

To Die Is Gain

In the second half of this verse, Paul says death is a gain, an advantage, for any Christian. Surely we would never take our own lives. We trust God to complete our physical lives in His time. Yet when the time comes, Christians can face death with joy and a longing for home. If you are a Christian, you know where you are going. You know who will be there when you arrive.

When my Uncle Marvin died, my Aunt Marjorie met me at the back door with a smile. When I gave her my condolences—and a casserole—she interrupted me with these words: "When I think of his joy . . . !" She beamed, thinking of Uncle Marvin in paradise. A good many years later my husband died, and then I understood. When someone who is one flesh with you goes to heaven, then half of you feels as if it's in heaven, and you can't help but rejoice when you think of the unspeakable joy of your loved one.

One day I'm going to that same place and will share that joy. I do not fear death. I look forward to heaven through the eyes of faith. What a wonderful transformation from mortal to immortal, from temporal to eternal, from weakness to strength, from imperfect to perfect, from death to life!

Look again at Philippians 1:21. For whom does Paul say this concept of life and death is true?

Paul could speak only for himself. He felt that Christ lived through him. You also can speak only for yourself. How do you feel about taking that concept into your heart?

Do you think the verse from Galatians below explains what Paul means in Phil. 1:21? Explain.

"I have been crucified with Christ and I no longer live, but Christ lives in me" (Gal. 2:20).

What will it mean for you to say, "To live is Christ"?

What will it mean for you to say, "To die is gain"?

The Mystery of Transformation: Through Christ We Live Forever

Paul says, "For as in Adam all die, so in Christ all will be made alive. Christ, the firstfruits; then . . . those who belong to him. . . . The last enemy to be destroyed is death" (1 Corinthians 15:22–23,26). We don't need to fear death; it's a normal part of life. Christ defeated death when he died—as a sacrifice for us—and then lived again. Instead of suffering eternal death when we die, we will join the resurrected Lord and be transformed to live eternally with Him. We die to live. Make sense? Not in the eyes of the world. Can't you see it, though? The mystery of transformation through eyes of faith.

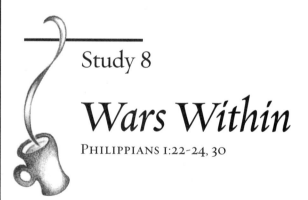

Study 8

Wars Within

PHILIPPIANS 1:22-24, 30

I ONCE WAS OFFERED A JOB IN A NEW LOCATION. THE SALARY was good, the work sounded exciting, and the people were nice. Several committees interviewed me, and they offered me the job. I told them I would let them know in a few days. That night in a hotel room they provided, I prayed and searched Scriptures for an answer. I wrote logical reasons for taking the job and an equal number of reasons for not taking it. True, the salary was good, but since it was a long way from my mother and the rest of my family, I'd spend the surplus flying home. Though the work sounded exciting, I wondered if I'd be worn out from all the excitement. Would I be exhausted from trying new things? While the people seemed nice, the supervisor had a special gleam in his eye that may have been meanness instead of genius. Could I trust him to be fair? I lay in bed for hours, pondering all these questions. Every half hour it was settled. I will take the job. Maybe. Or should I say no? Maybe no. Maybe yes. I beat the pillow to fluff it up and again went over the lists of pros and cons. Bleary-eyed the next morning, I decided nothing was worse than not being able to make up my mind.

Paul faced the same kind of dilemma. At times he wished he were out of jail. Even death would be better than his life, he may have thought. Then he remembered the good he was doing in jail, witnessing to the prison guards and influencing palace officials. He says, "If I am to go on living in the body, this will mean fruitful labor for me. Yet what shall I choose? I do not know! I am torn between the two: I desire to depart and be with Christ, which is better by far; but it is more necessary for you that I remain in the body" (Phil. 1:22–24).

Like Paul, I wrestled with my decision that night. Finally, I remembered a verse in Ecclesiastes: "The wise heart will know the proper time and procedure" (Ecclesiastes 8:5).

"But Lord, I'm not wise. That's why I need You." I was whining. (I complain and whine a lot with God. For a few years that was my main tone of communication with Him.)

Suddenly, another verse popped into my mind. "The fear of the LORD is the beginning of wisdom." As I sat silently, I remembered the second half of that verse: "And knowledge of the Holy One is understanding" (Proverbs 9:10).

As I drew close to God to learn more about His Word (this lasted about twenty minutes), I became impatient and said aloud, "Lord, I want an answer, and I want it now!"

Then a verse almost jumped off the page. "In the time of my favor, I will answer you" (Isaiah 49:8). I could almost hear Him say, "My favor, not yours, Edna!"

"Oops! Lord, I'm sorry. Take Your time. Uh . . . I can wait for the time of Your favor, not mine." Instead of becoming frantic

Friend to Friend

Have you ever wrestled for days with a decision?
☐ Yes, ☐ No

Are you facing one now? Explain.

Have you ever whined when you needed patience to understand God? Explain.

Have you ever impatiently asked God for something? Explain.

List the names of three or four people who may be watching your example.

because I did not have a definite answer, I just relaxed and went to sleep. In the morning God gave me a definite answer. I did not take the job, and it was a wise decision.

When I read Philippians, I do not see Paul whining, though he was in jail. Although Paul wrestled with both sides of this issue, he finally settled the matter. He says, "Convinced of this, I know that I will remain, and I will continue with all of you for your progress and joy in the faith, . . . since you are going through the same struggle you saw I had, and now hear that I still have" (Phil. 1:25,30).

When you struggle, others are watching. They want to know how you make it through the hard times of life. Sometimes God may allow you to go through a valley, so you can encourage others enduring the same struggle.

Doubt in the Heart

I know a woman who has belonged to every church in town. She is never satisfied, seeking the perfect situation, the perfect pastor, the perfect fellowship. She is never sure she has found what she is seeking. James says, "He who doubts is like a wave of the sea, blown and tossed by the wind. . . . He is a double-minded man, unstable in all he does" (James 1:6–7). You can eliminate doubt by trusting God to help you with decisions. Frantic rushing around and flitting from one place to another betrays doubt in the heart. You will make wise decisions that are steady and consistent when you seek God's Word and cheerfully live by God's direction. As you consistently depend on Him, your life reflects strength, not weakness, and confidence, not doubt.

Between a Rock and a Hard Place

I once walked into a counselor's office and nearly stumbled over an eighteen-inch square granite column on which was inscribed *Life Is Fair.*

"How did that rock get there?" I asked the counselor.

"One of my clients gave it to me," he said. "She kept complaining, 'But it's not fair!' and I usually retorted, 'Where is it chiseled in stone that life is fair?' One day she bought this granite column, had it chiseled with *Life Is Fair*, and dumped it here in my office. 'There!' she said. 'Don't ask me that question any more! *Here* is where it's chiseled in stone, *Life Is Fair*.'"

Is your back against the wall? Do you have hard decisions to make? Remember, you can depend on Jesus. You do not need a rock chiseled with *Life Is Fair*. Life is not fair, but God is your rock, your fortress, your deliverer, your salvation, and your stronghold (Psalm 18:2). He speaks to you through the psalmist: "I will praise the LORD, who counsels me; even at night my heart instructs me. I have set the LORD always before me. Because he is at my right hand, I will not be shaken. Therefore my heart is glad and my tongue rejoices; my body also will rest secure" (Psalm 16:7–9).

The Mystery of Transformation: Jesus Within Me, the Hope of Glory

Even in an imperfect world, when you have wars without and within, God offers steady consistency by which to live. With death, suffering, unfairness, and heartache all around you, God gives safety and peace. He can do what no one else can do: offer a solid rock to hold onto. He comes into your heart and lives within you, to quiet you, love you, and help you make wise decisions. In the middle of divorce, loss of job or family, and war outside, you can have peace and confidence inside. You can smile, hope, and bask in His glory. And that transformation is a mystery the world will marvel at!

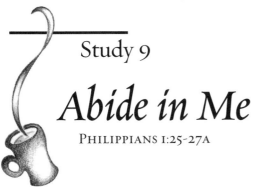

Study 9

Abide in Me

PHILIPPIANS 1:25-27A

SOMETIMES WE ABIDE IN STRANGE PLACES. IN 1999, I SERVED AS technical director for a large event held in a coliseum in Louisville, Kentucky—a job I had never done. Around 13,000 teenage girls gathered for NAC—National Acteens Convention—a Christian event for teenage girls from all over the world. You guessed it: these girls were not going to pay attention if the program was not lively.

My job was to make sure it hopped every minute. The sound had to be the right volume (too loud, of course, for me); the action on stage had to be projected on giant screens on top of the stage in the round. Thank goodness for the professional crew, who had done this many times. In one day, I got the hang of it: "Fade to camera five . . . great shot! Johnnie, raise the sound on that bass guitar . . . it's fading. Mark, the girl at entrance C took the mike. Get someone up there to place it back on mike stand nine for the African singers rushing in. Watch that spaceship! . . . Good. Spotlight needed at exit D! Fade to camera two." To tell the truth, I was so absorbed in keeping things going, I hardly paid attention to the wonderful action and message on stage.

Suddenly, I heard the entire audience singing the song "Change Me from the Inside Out." Girls were singing, hugging their friends, crying, and praying together. What a sight to see tens of thousands of young Christians praising God and singing "Change Me from the Inside Out." I found myself humming the song. That night, after the event was over, I sang the song over and over. The memory lingered on. So did the joy of that moment. I went to sleep that night, tired to the bone, but overflowing with joy.

Ongoing Faith

Paul was abiding in a strange place but overflowing with joy. He says, "Convinced of this, I know that I will remain, and I will continue with all of you for your progress and joy in the faith" (Phil. 1:25). He is convinced of "this" (that he is serving as an example by keeping his strong faith in Jesus his Savior, even in prison), and he needs to stay put, so they can progress in their Christian development. Hebrews 11:1 says, "Faith is the substance of things hoped for, the evidence of things not seen" (KJV). Your faith in God can be as certain as if you could reach out and touch the real substance of Him. Even though you have not seen Him through your physical eyes, you have seen the evidence that He is real through your spiritual senses.

Ongoing Joy

The result of Paul's great faith was that he believed his suffering helped Christians such as those in Philippi. He knew that if he saw them in the future, they would overflow with joy. He says, "So that

Can you remember a circumstance in which you could not see the whole picture and had to place your trust in God? Explain.

through my being with you again your joy in Christ Jesus will over-flow on account of me" (Phil. 1:26).

Read verse 25 aloud. In what is a Christian supposed to have joy?

Read verse 26 silently. In what else is a Christian supposed to have joy?

If a Christian has joy in *Christ* and joy in *the faith*, do you think these two verses differ from having *faith in Christ*? (Think more deeply through that idea.) Explain.

Friend to Friend

In what areas of your life do you need more joy?

How could placing Christ in that situation change it?

Ongoing Ongoing

Don't forget a key point in verse 25: Paul is suffering so the Philippians can progress; they will be encouraged not only to have joy but also to have perseverance. He might say today, "Keep on keeping on! Don't give up! God is good all the time—even when times are hard. Push forward! Don't be discouraged!"

And All Those Other Things

Paul says, "Whatever happens" (Phil. 1:27). He knows he is in real danger. He could die in this prison. He could focus on death and be depressed, but Paul chooses the things of God. He witnesses to anyone he meets in prison; as it turns out, some are influential people.

While traveling in Washington, D.C., with co-workers, we decided to visit Arlington Cemetery for two hours on Sunday morning and then rush back to Church of the Shepherd downtown. Later, in church, I realized my wallet was missing. I had left it on a bench in Arlington! I whispered the problem to Kathryn Kizer, and we stepped outside.

"Let's think this through," she said. "What could Satan throw in our paths to prevent us from worshipping this morning?"

"Fear of losing all my money—and my credit cards!" I said impatiently.

We decided to go back into the church, listen to the sermon, and then go look for the wallet at Arlington. I'm so glad I stayed! The pastor gave a remarkable sermon that morning. He said one sentence I'll never forget: "Remember, there's no such thing as a non-mess." In other words, if we wait for our lives to be free from messy circumstances, we'll never find our place of service in Christ. (I was so impressed that I have researched it and found that a "messy" universe is a scientific term. Scientists investigate incidents that don't fit laws of physics, the "messy" things that don't make sense—mysteries to the scientific world.)

I agree that the world is always in a mess in one place or another with war, poverty, or disease. Your life and mine will be a mess as long as we live on earth and not in heaven. All the housekeeping in the world cannot bring heaven on earth. The only place we find perfection is with almighty God in the eternal place called heaven.

By the way, one of the staff at Arlington found my wallet, and it was waiting for me, with all the money and cards, at the office.

Abiding Is Outside and Inside

In our country's capital I learned an important principle of godly living: "Seek first his kingdom and his righteousness, and all these things will be given to you" (Matt. 6:33). I learned that our outward behavior is a reflection of the peace and confidence inside, which grows from faith in Jesus Christ. Paul says it well: "Whatever happens, conduct yourselves in a manner worthy of the gospel of Christ. Then, whether I come and see you or only hear about you in my absence, I will know that you stand firm in one spirit, contending as one man for the faith of the gospel" (Phil. 1:27).

The Mystery of Transformation: Change Me from the Inside Out

How can our inner faith lead to outer confidence? It happens every day: a drunken husband, an abusive parent, a hateful sister, or a high-on-drugs teenager faces Jesus and totally changes. You may know someone like this. I do. He or she is absolutely transformed, and that is a mystery turned inside out!

Pray that your study partner will seek first God's kingdom and His righteousness in her life.

Study 10

Women with Solidarity

PHILIPPIANS 1:27b-29

IN STUDY 8 WE REFLECTED ON ONE OF PAUL'S REASONS FOR remaining in jail: "Whatever happens, conduct yourselves in a manner worthy of the gospel of Christ. Then, whether I come and see you or only hear about you in my absence, I will know that you stand firm in one spirit, contending as one man for the faith of the gospel" (Phil. 1:27). Paul serves as an example of standing firm in a time of trouble, hoping other Christians will also stand firm.

Flee the Fear

Verse 28 continues Paul's thoughts: "without being frightened in any way by those who oppose you." Paul certainly had reason to fear. Have you ever been deathly afraid?

In 1983, leading high school French students on a European tour, I tasted real fear. In Hamburg, Germany, I allowed my students to go (four at a time) with our translator to a disco in our hotel. At midnight, three girls reported that the translator had gone to bed and the fourth girl had gone to another disco with "older men." I was petrified.

I dressed and went out into the night to find her. I wandered around unknown streets, unable to speak German or find anyone who spoke English. I imagined myself saying to her father, "Yes, I know your daughter is a slave somewhere in the Middle East, but the last time I saw her she was in a disco in our hotel, under good supervision!" As I walked through a red-light district, I tasted something strange and metallic. I know it was the "substance of fear" in my mouth (in contrast to the substance of faith explained in Study 9). Within an hour I found the girl with the "older men," two eighteen-year-old American soldiers—young Christians, who looked as if they were thirteen. However, I kept my eye on her the rest of the tour, and I never let any student out of my sight. I don't ever want that fear again!

Paul could have been overcome by fear and so distracted by it that he sat and did nothing. He could have lived his days in prison according to the old saying, "Sometimes I sits and thinks, and sometimes I just sits." Instead, he took the offensive and triumphed. He allowed the Holy Spirit to shine through him into the lives of others. Since Paul was a Roman citizen, a well-educated man, and an articulate wordsmith, he probably strategized as he used his intelligence and influence to lead others to know Jesus. He probably assessed his assets and then planned ways to use them as tools to accomplish his goal: to introduce to a living Christ every unsaved person who came into that jail.

You and I can flee the fear. We can run from a condition of fear to a condition of faith and power to endure.

Who Are My Enemies?

Whether you admit it or not, nearly every woman has enemies. It's hard to suffer in silence when you've been mistreated. Having a history of lacking power, some of our foremothers learned to be manipulative to get what they needed. Because of that tradition and because of our cross-brained ability with relationships, many women today will attack, at the drop of a hat, those they see as unkind. Perhaps we don't realize when we do this. Being unafraid does not mean we should attack others. Paul says we should serve "without being frightened in any way by those who oppose" us (Phil. 1:28). Rather than showing a defensive attitude, taking sides, and dividing the church, Paul says we should stand in our faith "as one" (Phil. 1:27). If you are not standing as one with every woman in your church, decide today what you can do to become a woman of solidarity.

Together in Belief

Look at the end of verse 28: "This is a sign to them that they will be destroyed, but that you will be saved—and that by God."

What is "standing firm" a sign of?

To whom is it a sign?

When you refuse fear, stand firm, and show your faith, I believe it is a sign to your enemies (those who oppose you) that you will win, because Jesus has already won the victory. Who is watching you? Paul might say, "Mother, listen to your daughter. Sister, quit condemning. Daughter, forgive your mother. Fellow worker, love her despite her jealous behavior. Christian, see only good; be blind to evil you see in fellow Christians."

Lyle Shaller says that crisis is one thing that unites a church, in his book, *Strategies for Change* (Nashville, Abingdon Press, 1993, 48–49). I pray it will not take a crisis to do that in your area of influence.

Several years ago I listened to a man from China who had been persecuted for being a Christian pastor during the Cultural Revolution. An American missionary, Lottie Moon, had led his grandfather's family to know Christ, and the grandson had been a Christian for years. However, he spent many of those years in prison under the hardest of conditions. I wish you could have seen his face when he said (as I remember it), "Millions of Christians live in China today. The few who remained after World War II set such an example of faith as they suffered under the Japanese, that my generation knew we could do no less. I believe God allowed me to go to prison under the communists, so I could, like Paul, set an example for the generations that followed me."

Together in Suffering

Paul says, "For it has been granted to you on behalf of Christ not only to believe on him, but also to suffer for him" (Phil. 1:29). All of us suffer, sometimes because of our faith. People around you watch what you do. Some of them will be jealous of your joy when you accept Jesus as your Savior. (Sometimes the substance of faith in your mouth comes out in a smile or a silly grin they find obnoxious.) You may find that your best friends or family members can become your worst enemies. Isn't that incredible?

When my husband became a Christian, he delayed telling one of his close friends, because he knew he'd lose his friendship. That dear friend of many years stopped talking to my husband; he didn't

Friend to Friend

What do you say about other people?

Friend to Friend

Name a few people with whom you could improve your relationship. Explain.

hang around anymore. My husband was willing to witness and to suffer for Christ, but he dreaded it. Losing his good friend broke his heart. Imagine his joy when that friend later came into our kitchen, sat down, and asked my husband for help with a family problem. From then on, they were fast friends again, but first my husband had to go through a period of suffering.

The Mystery of Transformation: Joy in Suffering

During the worst suffering in life, a radiant Christian can find deep-down joy. How does that work? It defies every rule of common sense on this earth, but our Jesus can make the poor feel rich, the weak feel strong, and the sick feel healthy. Whatever you're suffering today, ask God to transform your sorrow into joy. Through a mysterious process beyond our understanding, He can change your life and give you victory over every enemy.

Unit 3:

Lord, I'm Dreaming High ... but Living Low

■ ■ ■ DURING THE 1930S, AN OKLAHOMA CHURCH struggled in a hard place. It was in a dry part of the state, so it had an inadequate water supply. The poor church members brought precious water from home whenever they met at church. Sermons and Bible studies focused on the pitiful condition of the church and its members. Finally the church folded. Twenty years later, a young pastor surveyed the place and brought church members from his congregation to start a mission. They dug for a well and found a clear underground spring a short distance down! Once they tapped into it, the new church flourished. It is still growing today.

Isn't it ironic that the first church never tried to dig a well? The water was close, yet so far away. As inheritors of eternal life, we should be the most joyful people on earth! We should tap into the Living Water and feel lifted up from the mundane, without selfishness, pride, strife, and fighting with others—or even within our own hearts. We don't need to search for anything but Jesus.

In this unit you can explore your relationship with your Lord and decide on ways you can drink from Him—and even overflow—with living water.

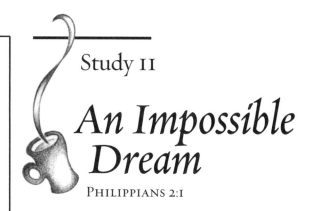

Study II

An Impossible Dream

PHILIPPIANS 2:I

How Jesus Woke Up and Went Up

Christianity is a simple concept. God created you and loved you. You are sinful, because all men and women are sinful; we drift away from Him. As a just God, He must punish sin, and therefore you deserve death (as all people do), if justice is served. However, He still loves you, so He wants to save you from death. He has a dilemma: how can He punish you with death and still save you for eternity? Simple answer: two thousand years ago He sent His Son to die in your place. Since Jesus died, you don't have to. All you have to do is accept this free gift of eternal life God gives you. He was resurrected (woke up) from death, and later He ascended (went up) to be with God in heaven. Because He lives after death, you can, too.

Why can't we see how simple this plan is? We live in a sinful world, where a free gift such as that seems impossible. In the musical *Man of La Mancha*, the novelist Cervantes, like Paul, is cast into prison. Yet he gives hope to the people there by telling them the story of the gentle knight Don Quixote. Don Quixote sees things differently than the world does. He treats and defends a prostitute as a lady, and she begins to show kindness and mercy to others, as a Christian knight's pure lady would do. In the end, Cervantes holds his head high as he walks to face death at the hands of the Spanish Inquisition, dreaming the impossible dream, fighting the impossible fight, having brought civility and hope to a brutal prison.

Listen to God's Spirit speaking to you through this verse: "Christ encourages you, and his love comforts you. God's Spirit unites you, and you are concerned for others" (Phil. 2:I CEV).

In what ways are you like Don Quixote?

Which of the things below are hardest for you to do?

☐ Find encouragement, not depression
☐ Find comfort in love that lasts
☐ Find a united spirit with everyone
☐ Find a genuine concern for ALL people

For most of us, these seem like an impossible dream. Let's look at them one at a time.

The Dream of Consolation

Paul says, "Christ encourages you" (Phil. 2:1 CEV). Circle one thing that encourages most women: man, husband, boyfriend, mother, father, aunt, uncle, sister, brother, career/job, home, car, children, dog, cat, church, friends, a drink, a smoke, food, chocolate, coffee, money in the bank/stock portfolio.

I once met a friend in a singles Bible study class who complained because God had left her single when all her friends had married young. "It's easy for you to be happy," Deb said, "because you have been married. God never gave me a husband." She left our class right after that.

A few years later I met Deb at the grocery store. She was newly married. I gave her my best wishes and rejoiced with her that she was happy. "Well," she said, "Greg is not perfect. I work really hard trying to please him, but he hasn't really made me happy. We're hoping to have a baby right away. I know that will help."

I cautioned her about expecting a baby to hold together a shaky marriage, urging her instead to become secure in her husband before a third family member came along. Two years later I saw her with a beautiful little girl. "You know," she said, "this child has brought us nothing but grief. Maybe siblings will help her not to be so selfish. She cries all the time and is so cranky; she's driving me crazy."

I have an idea that when Deb's children leave home, she'll complain about the silence driving her crazy, wishing she didn't have an empty nest. Deb will never be happy, because she's looking in all the wrong places. She needs to look to Christ, the source of all joy. Remember this: Relationships with a husband, a child, your mother, a best friend—or even chocolate—will not make you

What things are you counting on to make you happy?

What has Christ given you to make your life good?

Paul says, "His love comforts you" (Phil. 2:1).

What comforts you? Write several things besides relationships that make you smile when you think of them. Do you seek any of these when you seek comfort?

happy. If you are depressed and longing for deep joy, start with a relationship with Jesus.

The Dream of Comfort

My daughter, Patsy, and I were shopping in a very exclusive store. Suddenly, she said, "Mom, let's go!" I was still fingering a beautiful silk dress, but I followed her.

"What's the matter?" I said.

"I'm so disgusted. Everything in that shop is beyond my price range. It makes me sick to look at all these pretty things and know I'm denied them because of economics. I don't have enough money even to buy a scarf."

Patsy had just begun her first job, and she had to watch her pennies. Years later, after promotions and a good savings account, she surprised me when she did not spend her money on expensive clothes. I'm proud she has learned that clothes don't bring real comfort. Jesus does. As a lupus patient with fibromyalgia, she has learned that a day without pain brings great joy, dissolved blood clots cause a wide smile, and a benign report on a liver tumor can be ecstasy!

Shopping is an easy fix for pain, but nothing beats the comfort of knowing the Holy Spirit as your Comforter.

The Dream of Fellowship

You may dream the impossible dream of never being lonely. Nearly everyone has felt lonely in a crowd. My next-door neighbors habitually took other couples with them on vacation. One year no one could go with them, so they went alone. I waved good-bye to them at 8:00 AM, and at 4:00 PM they drove back into the driveway.

"What happened?" I asked.

"We couldn't stand it," they said. "The beach was lonely without friends." Sweating in my yard as I washed my car, I wished I had been going to the beach that day. What a waste of time, to drive three hours to the beach and return because of loneliness! Loneliness is the human condition. You long for home in heaven. Until you know Jesus, you will never know true satisfaction. You will always be lonely.

The Mystery of Transformation: The Dream of Mercy

Here is the good news: You can believe the free gift of salvation. God planned for all time to give you mercy, so if you're dreaming of that, be assured that heaven is a reality. You can exchange the impossible dream of a perfect human relationship, material comfort, and worldly satisfaction for the perfect consolation, comfort, and fellowship with God Himself! In His mercy, God transforms your life into a paradise beyond your wildest dreams. What a mystery!

Study 12

Same Ol', Same Ol'

PHILIPPIANS 2:2

DOLDRUMS ARE AREAS OF THE OCEAN NEAR THE EQUATOR WHERE the wind seldom blows. I've never been to the equator, but I've lived in the doldrums. Sometimes doldrums invade your home, your family, or your marriage. The expression "same ol', same ol'" described my life as a high school English teacher and yearbook sponsor. In those days before computers were common, we had to count words, being sure each column was 25 lines of 35 characters each. Long after my husband and children had gone to bed, I was up late, counting 1, 2, 3, 4 . . . 33, 34, 35/ 1, 2, 3, 4 . . . 33, 34, 35/ . . .

As I counted 25 slash marks (/), shortening or lengthening the articles for the yearbook, I often prayed, "Lord, I know a high school is a mission field—teens have many needs—but what am I doing counting characters late into the night?" A few years later, God gave me an awesome answer. After my husband died, a friend at church, a freelance writer, asked me to go to a writers' conference with her. "Are you kidding?" I laughed. "I promised myself that if I ever got out of school, I'd never write another paper for anyone!" (To tell the truth, I had promised myself I'd

What are the "same ol', same ol's" in your day today?

never read another book, either; I later found books more fun when I didn't have to read them for a book report.)

She said, "I need to go to this conference, but I can't afford to pay for a full room in a fancy hotel for a week. If I share the room, I can afford to go." She was a lovely Christian, and I wanted to help her, but I hesitated. I didn't have $600, my part of the cost. The hotel sounded luxurious, however, and I was tempted to go, so I told her I'd pray about it and see if it were possible. That week, as I cleaned out my husband's footlocker, I found a small envelope marked "Vacation." Inside was $600. I called my friend and said, "I'll go with you to the conference, but I probably won't go to many of the conferences. I do not want to be a writer; I just want to swim in the pool. I'm going on vacation." We decided to go.

After the first two days, I went to a conference on writing devotionals, thinking I may use a devotional idea in my church missions group's prayer time. After the conference, the leader asked me to turn in six devotionals for publication in a magazine for teenagers' daily quiet times. When I told my friend, she said, "Oh, Edna, you can't do that. When she mails you the specifications next week, you'll find devotionals are too hard. You'll write a good story, and then you'll have to cut half the words to fit a pattern, destroying the thoughts.

I was disappointed but waited for the instructions from the editor. Imagine my surprise when the specifications said, "Write 25 lines of 35 characters each." God had been training me for this writing assignment for years as a yearbook sponsor! With ease I polished off those six devotionals and eventually wrote over 400 of them. The extra income helped me to make it as a single parent. God had introduced me to the exciting world of writing, even as I dug in my high heels all the way! I never lived in the doldrums again.

Tropical depressions and inactivity live in the doldrums. If you are inactive in the same ol', same ol' periods of your life, you may experience depression, which invades your heart. Remember this: in the routine of the doldrums, God is training you for a new period of your life.

As unbelievable as it may seem, Paul asks the people at Philippi to do the same ol', same ol'. Paul ends the first verse of

Philippians 2 by reminding the people of Philippi that God's Spirit unites them and that their task is to be concerned for others. Then he writes, "Then make my joy complete by being like-minded, having the same love, being one in spirit and purpose" (Phil. 2:2). He calls them to joint sameness, and we'll explore in this chapter what he means.

Like a coach from a distant location, Paul urges them to do the right thing, to stand united, and to make him proud of them. His tone in these verses is like the tone of the famous coach who urged his team to "win one for the Gipper."

Of the Same Mind

His first instruction is to be like-minded. Don't you know God is pleased when a congregation can agree unanimously on *anything*?

Do you enjoy a good discussion in church?

Do you feel, like one of my friends, that you have the spiritual gift of criticism? (There is no such gift.)

Having the Same Love

Paul also asks the Philippians to have the same love. Explain what you think "same love" means.

Choose one of the following to describe which kind of love you most often feel when you relate to fellow church members or dear friends:

☐ Eros—sexual love; lust you feel for a lover

☐ Philos—brotherly love; companionship you feel for a sibling or friend

☐ Agape—unselfish love; reverence you feel for God.

God calls us to agape love for all people—our friends, our family, and the most unlovely person you know. How could you show that kind of love to an unlovely and unloving person? Can you have the same ol', same ol' love for an unlovely person, just as you have for your most lovely friend?

List ways you can help your congregation have a more peaceful spirit and be of the same mind.

In what way will you submit to Christ?

Friend to Friend

One in Purpose

One Christmas when I was a little girl I read the story "The Gift of the Magi." In this classic story by O. Henry, a newly-married husband and wife with little money wanted to buy each other a special Christmas present. The woman sold her beautiful hair, which many people admired, to buy a watch chain for her husband's prized pocket watch. At the same time, the husband sold his prized watch to buy decorative combs for her beautiful hair. Their purpose was the same: to show agape love to each other. Jesus, in the perfect agape love, gave the most unselfish gift, Himself, for us. Can we give any less to Him?

In the Same Joy

Playing a character filled with malice, Clint Eastwood said, "Make my day." Filled with love, Paul said, "Make my joy complete." He uses "joy" eighteen times in this letter to his friends in Philippi. Since joy, not depression or despair, is the theme of this letter, we sometimes forget a prisoner wrote it. Paul would have wanted it that way.

The Mystery of Transformation: Doldrums Turn to Va-va-va-voom!

In Study 11, we discussed bored people who were dissatisfied without friends. They tried to escape the same ol', same ol' humdrum of life. Christians may say they don't want to think like, act like, or feel like their fellow Christians, but nothing is more exciting than being a part of a Christian fellowship that moves out together with the mind of Christ! Like the warm doldrums near the equator that spawn the powerful winds of a hurricane, you, when willing to join forces with God's people, can be a part of awesome power bigger than the universe.

The "Other" Principle

PHILIPPIANS 2:3-4

AS A CHILD I LEARNED THIS ACROSTIC FOR RELATING TO OTHERS:
   J-Jesus first
   O-Others second
   Y-Yourself third
It helped me to think of others, which is not an easy concept for a mean little girl who wanted to be first in everything.

Paul says, "Don't be jealous or proud, but be humble and consider others more important than yourselves. Care about them as much as you care about yourselves" (Phil. 2:3–4 CEV).

What two things does Paul ask you not to be? _____ and _____.

What three things does Paul ask you to do? _____, _____, and _____.

"Other-ing" and What It Means

Earlier in this study we learned what "under-ing" means. Under-ing describes your vertical relationship with Jesus, who says in Matthew 22:37, "Love the Lord your God with all your heart and with all your soul and with all your mind." Other-ing describes your horizontal relationship with others: "Love your neighbor as yourself" (Matt. 22:39). Loving others is important to God. Our love for God is acted out in the way we love others. Jesus says, "All the Law and the Prophets hang on these two commandments" (Matt. 22:40).

Two women in my sister's Bible study class portray the under-ing and other-ing combination when they visit unchurched neighbors. They pray, asking God to lead them, and then they visit people who don't know Him. They identify needs and

Write here what "under-ing" means to you.

Circle the places below where you can practice under-ing and other-ing:

In my neighborhood

In my church

At the funeral home

In my civic club

At school

At home

At a relative's home

Circle any ideas in these quotations that you have heard in your life.

Explain to your study partner how you felt when you heard these words.

demonstrate love as they meet the needs. On their church's regular visitation night, when I ask, "Where are you going tonight?" they reply, "We're under-ing and other-ing!"

The opposite of the "other-ing" principle may be jealousy. Jealousy is the drive to get ahead of others. Sometimes it centers on one person.

Jealousy Leads to Selfishness

My mother always made it clear that she wanted my life to be easier than hers. She tried to provide things for me that she never had: good shoes, nice sweaters, a clean house, a warm heater, and a comfortable bed. (In her day, living in the country, they had cold rooms and tiny bedbugs in the children's cornshuck mattresses.) Mother often denied herself for her children. She wore the same faded dress to church so we could have new clothes. She did our chores occasionally so we could go to a birthday party. She exhibited Christian kindness every day.

One of my classmates' mothers seemed jealous of her daughter. She made remarks such as

• "Well, you're no better than I was. I did this when I was your age."

• "Who do you think you are, a princess? You get to work and help me. I never had any fun in my life! I've always worked hard."

• "You are certainly not buying a new car—and you're not riding in my new Cadillac with your sticky fingers."

My friend's mother was jealous of her daughter, not providing anything for her children that she did not first have. She had a deep-down drive to put self above all else—above all others.

Jealousy Leads to Pride

In the drive to become better than anyone else, people begin to fill their hearts with pride. Jealousy works like a seesaw: for you to be up, another person must be put down. Insults and name-calling are tools God uses to identify the jealousy in your heart.

If you feel threatened by someone, you might demonstrate bravado (a false sense of self-importance) to prove you are better than the other person. In truth, we wish we were as powerful as the one who threatens us, and we are jealous of him or her. Therefore, we try to be better, bigger, and brighter than the other person. Many of us behaved this way as children. (We still may sometimes revert to this behavior when we are around our sisters and/or brothers, because they remind us of our childhood.)

When you mature as a Christian, you have a deep well of love, allowing you to share with others and show unselfishness, as Jesus did. The more you take on His character, the less jealous you are. You will truly love and respect yourself, because you know He loves you. Then you can love and respect others.

Jealousy Leads to Strife

You can become a diva, a queen bee. You know the type: a woman who demands (not commands) devotion from her family. Her husband must follow her lead, her children do without certain things because their mother thrives on luxury for herself. Outside the home, she must be the center of activity. She becomes the queen bee of every gathering: president of every club, star of every performance, and leader of every group. No one likes a queen bee—a selfish, backstabbing, all-ruling person. When you fall into the queen bee syndrome, you *will* have strife with others. Maybe today you can think of a situation of strife in your life. Paul asserts that you can do something about it. He urges, "Don't be jealous or proud, but be humble and consider others more important than yourselves. Care about them as much as you care about yourselves" (Phil. 2:3–4 CEV).

The Mystery of Transformation: The Queen Bee Becomes a Worker

Even Christians fall into the trap of jealousy and pride, because these are natural human characteristics. Even if your natural tendency is to demand attention and to be jealous of others, God can mysteriously change you into a worker bee for Him. Only through under-ing, that is, submitting your personality and will to Him, can you do what He wants you to do. Believe this mystery: because God loves you, you can begin the joy of other-ing.

Friend to Friend

Describe some silly name-calling you did in your childhood.

Did it hurt someone?

Describe some ways jealousy has hindered your maturity.

Study 14

Low and Lowly

PHILIPPIANS 2:5-8

HAVE YOU EVER NEEDED A HULA HOOP FOR A HEADBAND? You might as well admit it. All of us occasionally have a swelled head about being so swell. Occasionally I fall into this trap: I do something well and begin to pat myself on the back a little too enthusiastically. For instance, one day I played golf with friends on a perfect morning. The temperature was perfect; we played on the perfect golf course (a short par three is always nice) with beautiful flowers and manicured greens. On one tee, I hit the perfect shot, using the perfect swing. The ball sailed into the air, arched at just the right height, and plopped within two feet of the hole. As I picked up my tee and walked to the green, I felt sorry for those untalented slobs playing with me. "You know," I said to myself, "you may be called the Nancy Lopez of the millennium."

I walked taller and slimmer. The air seemed a little fresher, and as I breathed deeply, I imagined I could see in the distance a talent scout for the pros. I could hardly wait for my next shot. While others were putting, I could almost hear the crowd cheering in expectation of my championship putt. Then, when it was my turn, I hit the worst shot imaginable. The putter went off in my hand like a trigger-happy pistol, and I overshot the hole—why, I even overshot the green! My ball rolled slowly off the opposite side and into the high grass in the woods.

"How could I?" I asked myself, throwing my putter down. "I'll never play golf again. I'm sick of this stupid game!" We had only one more hole to play, so I endured for the sake of the others. Yet on the next hole, I swung and voila! What a shot! It was better than Beth Daniels and Nancy Lopez put together! "That settles it. I'll go pro next week. I *am* good at this fabulous game."

Just as I sunk the last magnificent putt, I hit a clinker that sailed off into the woods again, missing by a mile! "Why does God always have to humble me?" I whined. Today I have an answer to that question. I needed to learn how to remain in an attitude of servanthood. God frequently reminds me about my position of servant as He nudges me in the right direction—under His wing, not three miles ahead of Him, directing the world.

The Mind of Jesus, Our Example

Philippians 2:5–8 echoes what we learned in Study 1 about under-ing: we can find joy in humility. Paul says, "Your attitude should be the same as that of Christ Jesus: Who, being in very nature God, did not consider equality with God something to be grasped, but made himself nothing, taking the very nature of a servant, being made in human likeness. And being found in appearance as a man, he humbled himself and became obedient to death—even death on a cross!" (Phil. 2:5–8). What a transforma-tion! Our Lord became more humble than we can imagine, giving up all the joys of life in heaven for death on earth. If we have the same attitude (v. 5), we can experience the very mind of Christ.

At age sixty-five, my grandmother bought a car and learned to drive. My grandfather, who did not drive, always told my grandmother how to drive. She once said of him, "He is willing to take a back seat, but he insists on being a back-seat driver!" It's hard for any of us to be humble enough to take a back seat and let our Lord drive.

Handmaid to the Lord

Even the mother of Jesus had to take a back seat in the kingdom occasionally. Imagine what it must have been like for this humble teenager to see an angel, Gabriel, who told her she would have a child, Jesus, the Son of God. Read Luke 1:26–38, and think about how you would have responded.

Choose the answers below that apply to you:
☐ If this had happened to me, I would have been scared out of my sandals!
☐ I'm pretty brave. No angel would have scared me.
☐ I would never have trusted someone named Gabriel.
☐ I would never have believed the story about a pregnant virgin.
☐ I would have said, "No way, Jose," and run to the nearest exit.

In what ways are you a back-seat driver?

Perhaps the angel gave Mary courage when he told her, "Nothing is impossible with God" (v. 37). Though she must have been confused by this awesome message, she believed his words. Notice that Mary submitted to God's will for her life. Luke 1:38 gives her response: "I am the Lord's servant. . . . May it be to me as you have said," or "Behold, the bondslave of the Lord; be it done to me according to your word" (NASB). Mary uses the same word, "servant" (NIV), or "handmaid" (KJV), or "bondslave" (NASB), as Paul uses in the first verse of Philippians.

Chosen One, Not Cast Away

God says, "As you come to him, the living Stone—rejected by men but chosen by God and precious to him—you also, like living stones, are being built into a spiritual house. . . . You are a chosen people" (1 Peter 2:4–5,9). God chose Mary to be the mother of Jesus. God called her to bring Him into the world in a manger, a humble birthplace. God also calls you to be a handmaiden of the Lord. Like Mary, you are precious to God and called to be His servant, or bondservant. In a world of bondage to all sorts of perversions and sin, what a privilege to be in bondage to our Lord!

We may be called to a lowly place, just as Paul and Mary were called. Yet each of these was raised up as an example of one who served regardless of the risk. A woman should not let anyone continue to abuse her, but she can trust almighty God not to do that. You can trust Him to guide your life, even when He brings you to a low point. He has a reward in heaven for His servants.

The Mystery of Transformation: The Divine Son Is the Suffering Servant

Pastor Dan Yeary went to visit his mentor and former pastor who was in pain, ill with cancer. To Dan's surprise, his mentor said, "Dan, I just want you to know that Jesus Christ is sufficient. Even now, I am happy in Him. Not only do I *like* Him but [also] I want to *be like* Him." This godly man had met Jesus face to face and was willing to follow Him even in suffering. Jesus, our divine Lord, was transformed into a suffering Servant. Why did He do it? Because He loves you. And that is no mystery.

How can you identify with Mary?

When can a person become too lowly?

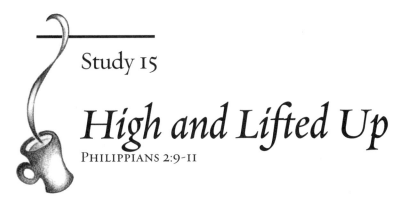

Study 15

High and Lifted Up

PHILIPPIANS 2:9-11

IN STUDY 14 WE DISCUSSED THE ABSOLUTE HUMILITY OF Christ, that He humbled himself and became obedient to death— even the humiliating death on the cross. Paul, himself in a lowly position in a Roman prison, continued to come back to the theme of obedience and under-ing—humbling yourself to walk under Christ's wing. He says, "Therefore [that is, because Jesus humbled himself and was obedient even to death] God exalted him to the highest place and gave him the name that is above every name, that at the name of Jesus every knee should bow, in heaven and on earth and under the earth, and every tongue confess that Jesus Christ is Lord, to the glory of God the Father" (Phil. 2:9–11).

How would you like to be exalted?

If I Be Lifted Up

Jesus said, "And I, if I be lifted up from the earth, will draw all men unto me" (John 12:32 KJV). Notice the first step to being humble and obedient is to place yourself under Christ's authority. We do that by lifting up Christ. Perhaps a Bible scholar would say that "lifted up" refers to Jesus' ascension into heaven. It is true that only through His death and resurrection are you drawn with Him into heaven, but these words are also symbolic. If you lift Him up, placing yourself lower than He is, He will call you to Him. Listen to these words from Isaiah 66:2: "This is the one I esteem: he who is humble and contrite in spirit, and trembles at my word." How long has it been since you trembled when you read God's word?

I Will Call All Men Unto Me

Here is another of the Bible's paradoxical passages: when you lower yourself, Jesus raises you up. When you humble yourself, willing to walk in darkness for Him, He glorifies you in His light.

Notice where Jesus is when He calls you to be with Him. "God exalted him to the highest place" (Phil. 2:9). He is at the right hand of God, forever exalted! Karla Worley, a woman I admire greatly, says her son often sings, "He is exhausted, the king is exhausted on high!" (Actually, Karla confesses that she is the poster child for exhausted women—and she wrote a book about her experiences, called *Growing Weary Doing Good*). Our God never grows weary. He is exalted but never exhausted!

The Name of Jesus

Paul clearly states that God gave His Son the name that is above every name, Jesus. Janella Griggs, a new friend who loves Hispanic people, told me she is convinced that Jesus must have been Spanish—or else why would God have given Him the name Jesus (she pronounces it HAY-soos)!

Most earthly parents seek just the right name for their children, making sure the children will earn respect because of the name. In Jesus' day, a name was even more important than it is today. It was a blessing or a curse on your life. If you had lived in those days and your father had named you Outcast, then no one would speak to you. If you were named Gentle, then you grew to be a gentle-spirited person. You literally became your name. In 1 Chronicles, Jabez's mother named him Pain because of a difficult childbirth, and everyone expected him to be filled with pain. He prayed, asking God to bless him, to enlarge his territory, and not to allow him to be in pain or cause pain to others (1 Chronicles 4:9-10).

Paul says that the name of Jesus is above every other name. (That means we are below; there's that under-ing theme again.) At Jesus' name, without His even being there, people will bow and acknowledge Him as Lord.

Can you hear the Hallelujah Chorus ringing in your ears as you read this passage? These words are majestic. At the name of Jesus, not only the Christians but everyone will bow. In what three places will this happen?

1. In heaven, in hell, and on the moon
2. In heaven, on the earth, and under the earth
3. In heaven, at the king's throne, and at the last supper

The psalmist says, "Let the heavens rejoice, let the earth be glad; let the sea resound, and all that is in it; let the fields be jubilant, and everything in them. Then all the trees of the forest will sing for joy; they will sing before the LORD, for he comes" (Psalm 96:11–13).

Eugene Peterson translates this verse in Philippians as, "God lifted him [Jesus] high and honored him far beyond anyone or anything, ever, so that all created beings in heaven and on earth—even those long ago dead and buried—will bow in worship before this Jesus Christ, and call out in praise that he is the Master of all, to the glorious honor of God the Father" (Phil. 2:9–11 *The Message*).

Explain how you think fields can be jubilant and trees can sing, as the Psalmist describes.

How can you be jubilant and sing?

Friend to Friend

The Mystery of Transformation: Power in the Name

After an American golfer played a benefit in a Middle Eastern country, the king insisted on giving him an extravagant gift, such as a car, a house, etc., but the golfer refused. Finally, at the king's insistence, the golfer agreed to accept a small gift, perhaps a golf club. Later a man handed the golfer a set of keys. "No," said the golfer, "I won't take a car or a house." The king's ambassador answered, "It's not a car or a house. It's a golf club. These are the keys to the clubhouse and all the outbuildings, signed for by the king!" The moral to the story: Be careful what you ask for in the presence of the King. There's mysterious, transforming power in His glorious name.

Unit 4:

Lord,
I Know I Need to Get Real

■ ■ ■ ■ WHILE YOU EXPLORE WHO YOU ARE IN CHRIST, walking with Him and trying to dream high, a day comes, as it does for each of us, when you know you have got to get real. Instead of pretending that the Christian life is a piece of cake, you wipe that plastic smile off your face and tell the truth. It is hard to live the Christian life. Deep-down joy can be buried under a pile of junk. The evil one causes you to stumble. For goodness' sake, your family and friends give you grief! Worse yet, wars within your heart may cause you to trip and fall along the way.

Be assured, fellow Christian, God knows your struggle. He holds you up when you do not realize it. You can relax and be real. In Unit 4, you will explore the reality of submission and obedience. You will look at what it means to stand in the middle of your enemies and speak the truth in love. You'll even hear a true angel story! In the midst of real sacrifice, you can rejoice as you study His holy word from Philippians. Ask your Lord to come alongside you and help you and your friend study this unit. You know the routine by now: turn the page and begin!

Study 16

Obedience Is Too Long and Too Hard

PHILIPPIANS 2:12-13

THIS STUDY INCLUDES THE DREADED O-WORD: OBEDIENCE. Along with patience, obedience is one of the hardest virtues to attain. Paul says to his friends in Philippi, "Therefore, my dear friends, as you have always obeyed—not only in my presence, but now much more in my absence—continue to work out your salvation with fear and trembling, for it is God who works in you to will and to act according to his good purpose" (Phil. 2:12–13).

Scholars have argued for years over the meaning of these verses, because they seem to indicate that you can earn your salvation by doing good works. When I was a little girl, I thought God had a scale on which He weighed our sins and good deeds on Judgment Day. If our sins outweighed the good things we did, we went to hell. If our good deeds outweighed our sins, we went to heaven. But my theory was wrong. Good works are the result, not the cause, of our salvation. Because Jesus became the sacrificial Lamb for our sins, we simply accept His free gift and receive eternal life. Paul says, "For it is by grace you have been saved, through faith—and this not from yourselves, it is the gift of God—not by works, so that no one can boast" (Eph. 2:8–9).

So you say, "Jesus, I trust You and You alone for my salvation. I accept You as my Savior and Lord." As you become spiritually mature, you learn that sometimes you have to obey whether or not you feel good, whether or not you sense His glorious presence in your life at that moment. Remember, Paul says his friends have obeyed in his presence and much more in his absence.

I once heard a missionary say that while bullets whizzed over the heads of several couples and small children hiding in a hallway under mattresses, they could not pray. They could not feel God's presence in that war-torn land. They were too scared

Have you ever felt that God was absent to you? Explain.

to sense Him. Though they were comforted by knowing someone was praying for them, they did not feel God's presence until two days later. I was disillusioned by her testimony. I thought if a godly missionary doubted God, then I, who was not so godly, had no hope. I wanted to hear a story with a Cinderella ending, where outer circumstances brought happiness.

Since then, I've matured in my walk with God, and I know He loves me no matter how godly I am. Nothing I do can make Him love me less. I know I can trust God even when I can't feel His presence every moment. Even with that assurance, I've still felt pain and experienced desperate times of questioning God's goodness. Get real! It's hard to obey over the long haul in desperate circumstances.

When you face job loss, divorce, death of a child or parent, unfair suffering, or (you fill in the blank), you can't help but cry out, "O God, I didn't sign on for this! I didn't know life would be so hard!" I read an email story recently that echoes that sentiment. The late comedienne, Gracie Allen, received all sorts of gifts from her fans. One day someone left an alligator at her house. Mrs. Allen found it later in the bathtub with a note from the maid, who had quit, saying, "I don't do alligators." At times I would like to say, "Lord, I quit. I don't do rebellious teenagers. I don't do a husband's death. I don't do single parenting. I don't do miscarriages."

My Point of Hurt

Here is a spiritual principle I have found valid in my life and the life of every Christian I know: the point of your deepest hurt is the point at which God can use you most to encourage others. If you have experienced childlessness, you can help another woman walk through that dark valley. If you've experienced sexual abuse, you can help someone overcome her past and find spiritual wellness. Only one who has grieved can help someone overcome grief. You can help someone find her way only if you've walked that way before. Think now of your worst humiliation or hurt. Can you be real enough with someone to show her the way, to overcome, to feel the presence of God by sharing that with her?

Oh dear one, do you read these words with fear and trembling? Listen again to Paul's words: "as you have always obeyed—

List some things you wish you could tell God that you "don't do."

Write one thing you may share with your Bible study partner to encourage her.

not only in my presence, but now much more in my absence—continue to work out your salvation with fear and trembling, for it is God who works in you to will and to act according to his good purpose" (Phil. 2:12–13). God works in you, offering salvation first when you trust Him and then helping you to have the firm will to act according to His purpose, not yours. His purpose is always good. He will never violate you. He will have only good gifts for you, including heaven.

In 1937, Charles Williams translated Philippians 2:12 this way, "So now with reverence and awe keep on working clear down to the finishing point of your salvation." Paul says to other church friends, "Let us not become weary in doing good" (Gal. 6:9) and "Never tire of doing what is right" (2 Thess. 3:13). Eugene Peterson translates Philippians 2:12 this way, "Be energetic in your life of salvation, reverent and sensitive before God. That energy is *God's* energy, an energy deep within you, God himself willing and working at what will give him the most pleasure" (Phil. 2:12–13 *The Message*). When the burdens are heavy and you feel alone, remember God's energy for you, to tap into.

What experiences give you God's energy?

The Too-Heavy Burdens

You may take heart with a fresh energy while reading the words above. However, you may hurt too much to believe them. If you are burdened, listen to these words: "Do you not know? Have you not heard? The LORD is the everlasting God, the Creator of the ends of the earth. He will not grow tired or weary" (Isaiah 40:28). "He tends his flock like a shepherd: He gathers the lambs in his arms and carries them close to his heart" (Is. 40:11). God cares about your burdens, and He has the energy to handle them.

The Mystery of Transformation: His Good Pleasure Brings Me Pleasure

During the darkest days of my life, I have felt total spiritual wellness in spite of the circumstances. When you grieve, ask the King of kings to give you pleasure. When you lack peace, ask the Prince of Peace to give it. When you are angry, ask for the Holy Spirit's love. When you are tired, ask for energy from the Creator. I do not understand it, but I know that God gives pleasure while He works within, transforming you as you do His good pleasure.

Study 17

What Are Murmurings and Disputings?

PHILIPPIANS 2:14

THE WORD "MURMUR" HAS ALWAYS FASCINATED ME. SAY IT quickly three times aloud, and hear the murmuring sound. Poetry students recognize "murmur" as onomatopoeia, a poetic device in which a word sounds like its meaning. For instance, the word "gong" resonates and rings low, like a large round gong, and "piccolo" has the high, crisp sound of the flute. Other words also sound like their meanings. Think of flashing words from the old Batman television show: "Bam!" "Zap!" "Va-room!" All these words make sounds. Now say "dispute" as loudly as you can. "Dispute" may sometimes be onomatopoeia. You can hardly say this word without hissing and pushing out your lips angrily. Do you agree? Say "dispute" again with a snarl. No matter which word seems more friendly or likeable, neither murmuring nor disputing is likeable behavior.

When You Murmur

Paul says, "Do all things without murmurings and disputings" (Phil. 2:14 KJV). Webster's says murmuring is "An indistinct complaint." Today we might say, "Do everything without *complaining* or *arguing*" (Phil. 2:14 emphasis added). Remember, Paul is writing these words to church members. Why should he need to say these things to Christians?

Servants That Are Obedient but Blind

As he wrote the letter to the church members at Philippi, Paul may have been thinking of this verse from Isaiah: "Who is blind but my servant? . . . Who is blind like the one committed to me? . . . You . . . have paid no attention; your ears are open, but you

Try this activity: ask your Bible study partner and your family to tell you which word (*murmur* or *dispute*) they like best and why. Record their answers below.

Which word did they like the best? Which word did they like the least?

hear nothing" (Is. 42:19–20). Sometimes even committed Christians can read or hear the right words but not get the right message.

A highway patrolman stopped a man in a car filled with penguins. "Sir," said the highway patrolman, "you can't ride around with a car full of penguins. Take them to the zoo."

"Okay," the man said, and he drove away.

The next day the highway patrolman saw the same man with a car full of penguins. This time all of them had on sunglasses. "Sir," said the highway patrolman, "didn't I tell you to take these penguins to the zoo?"

"Yes, sir," said the man, "and thank you for that suggestion yesterday. We had so much fun at the zoo that today we decided we'd go to the beach!"

The man with the penguins heard the right words but he missed the message completely. Like him, we often hear the words God tells us, but we miss the message He is trying to convey.

The Real Murmurings God Hears

Sometimes we can't hear the message God sends us because we are too busy complaining about our lives. We are never satisfied with Jesus. We want Jesus in our hearts, but we also want a perfect life, no pain or death, a Prince Charming husband, protection for our children . . . and the list goes on.

The Real Disputings Your Rivals Hear

Do Christians have rivals? ☐ Yes ☐ No
Do Christians have rivals who are fellow church members? ☐ Yes ☐ No

Would you consider anyone your rival?
☐ Yes ☐ No

Would anyone consider you her rival?
☐ Yes ☐ No

If they do not hear clearly what God says to them, women who are fellow church members with rivalry and friction between them can tear a church apart. If you or your study partner/prayer partner can identify anyone you think is a rival, ask God to show you what she thinks of you. How can you change that image?

Women Who Divide Churches

Years ago someone told me that women are either aggressors or repressors. You may know someone with the aggressive, Type A personality, who steamrolls over everyone she meets. She is always right and won't listen to anyone. You may also know the repressor, with a Type B personality, who will do anything to avoid confrontation. She becomes a doormat and accepts bad treatment.

Some people—perhaps members of your church—handle their anger by becoming an aggressor. If someone says an unkind or hurtful word, aggressors explode. They shout, storm around the room, and threaten. Their anger calls for physical action. Others may handle their anger by becoming a repressor. Repressors react to anger by shrinking away from an angry, hurtful person. They say little as they joke, cajole, or smile at the angry person. Their inner anger calls for peace. They will acquiesce even if they do not agree in their hearts, just to end the volatile situation. Repressors are not better Christians than aggressors just because they keep their nasty words to themselves. God knows every heart.

I believe a third type of person exists: a spiritually mature Christian who has a *confessor* reaction to anger. This person confesses to God her exploding anger. Aggressors and repressors can both become confessors who handle their anger in a proper way. If the confessor has a naturally *aggressive* personality, she may say, "Lord, You know that I want to punch that person's lights out. Help me speak the truth in love, so she knows how I feel without me making a fool of myself with uncontrollable anger. Above all, Lord, do not let the sun go down on my anger." If the confessor has a naturally *repressive* personality, she may say, "Lord, You know that person just made me want to cry. Help me speak the truth in love. Give me the courage to talk to her face and not behind her back. Above all, Lord, do not let the sun go down without my expressing my true feelings. Don't let me keep my anger within my heart and pretend it's not there."

Just Do It!

We all feel angry sometimes, but we can acknowledge the anger before God, handle it in an honest way, and live a Christian life without murmuring and disputing. Paul says, "For we are God's workmanship, created in Christ Jesus to do good works, which

Which type are you most like, aggressor or repressor?

God prepared in advance for us to do" (Eph. 2:10). God planned wonderful things for you to do and prepared you to do them. You can't fulfill His perfect plan for your life when you waste yourself on insignificant situations or fill yourself with an attitude of getting ahead, getting angry, and getting even.

James 1:26 says, "If anyone considers himself religious and yet does not keep a tight rein on his tongue, he deceives himself and his religion is worthless." When it comes to murmuring, disputing, complaining, arguing, whining, cajoling, sniveling, cursing, fighting, slandering, gossiping, lying, maligning, or writhing in wrath, just say no!

The Mystery of Transformation: Jesus Tames My Tongue

Have you ever said anything that surprised you? As you talked with others, did an ugly, hurtful, or profane word pop out of your mouth? You wish you could have taken it back, but it was too late. Today you may know you need to control your tongue, but your resolve doesn't always work. James 3:8 says, "Nobody can tame the tongue." If you are a Christian, you know Someone who can control your tongue: Jesus. Instead of saying, "Shut my mouth," ask Him for the mystery of transformation in your heart and tongue.

Study 18

Here I Stand in the Middle of the Wolves

PHILIPPIANS 2:15

AT AGE TWENTY-TWO, PAM SMITH BECAME A TWO-YEAR missionary volunteer to Jordan. She and a fellow volunteer, Sherry, decided to take a vacation in Kenya. Returning from safari, they found Nairobi under a coup. Rebels had taken over the government and controlled all means of transportation, including the airport. All missionaries in Pam's denomination had fled except one man and his pregnant wife, who was in the hospital.

Sherry flew out the next day, but officials told Pam to check for tickets the following day. Alone in a guesthouse on the missionary compound, Pam spent a fearful night waiting for the dawn. For hours she prayed, "Lord, I'm really afraid. I know You will take care of me, but Lord, I am scared." The next morning the missionary took her to the airport, left her on the curb, and rushed back to the hospital. With hundreds of others, Pam waited four hours in a long line to get tickets. She felt even more alone, since she was the only white American in a crowded sea of Africans. She kept glancing over her shoulder for machine guns or any anti-American sentiment. She had no friend, no one who looked like her.

Finally, at the ticket counter, the agent asked, "Are you two traveling together?" Confused, Pam turned around and found a young woman about her age with light brown hair, who said, "Yes, we'd like to sit together, please."

Pam was speechless. She had been looking over her shoulder all day and had not seen this American. She boarded the plane with the stranger, who introduced herself as Mary. She told Pam she was backpacking around the world. During the four-hour flight to Cairo, Egypt, Mary talked about Jesus. She encouraged Pam with words such as, "Isn't our Lord wonderful? Even in the midst of war in a strange country, we can depend on Him. God is good, isn't He? Every time I need Him, He's always there." Pam began to relax and enjoy the flight, looking into the comforting eyes of Mary, who seemed totally serene as she talked of Him.

In Cairo, they deplaned down the steep steps. Pam had a connecting flight home, but Mary's destination was Cairo. As they got ready to say goodbye, Pam realized she had some Egyptian money she would not have time to spend in the airport. Offering it to Mary, she set her two carry-on bags down long enough to get the bills out of her pocket. Pam reached for the money, but Mary was gone.

"Edna," Pam told me later, "we were standing on the tarmac, a long way from any door into the airport. There's no way

Identify the things Paul suggests we become in Phil. 2:15.

she could have gone inside—or back on[to] the plane—in that instant. I believe I was in the presence of an angel. What do you think?"

Pam and I agreed that sometimes God protects us most dramatically when we are most afraid. In the midst of wolves, the Good Shepherd safeguards His sheep.

Blameless But Not Harmless

In Study 17 we learned that through Christ we can do everything without complaining or arguing. In this study we will discover that Paul gives us a reason for avoiding an argument or complaint. He says, "So that you may become blameless and pure, children of God without fault in a crooked and depraved generation, in which you shine like stars in the universe" (Phil. 2:15).

Paul suggests we become *blameless* and *pure*. "Pure" is translated "harmless" (KJV), "innocent" (NASB), and "spotless" (Williams). Have you ever been pure, harmless, innocent, or spotless? (I was spotless for about five minutes once when I had on a brand new dress!) Paul is speaking of spiritual purity. You know that on your own, you can never be totally pure or innocent. If you have ever been around a baby, you know they are born in a state of selfishness and need. By the time they are in the "terrible twos," they scream for someone to meet all their needs and are not willing to share anything with anybody. (At two, my children's favorite word was "No!")

Yet verse 15 says we are to be "*children of God*, without fault in a crooked and depraved generation" (emphasis added).

Me? A Daughter of God?

At this moment you may not feel like a child of God. Even strong Christians feel far away from Him occasionally—when they are angry, when they have done something wrong, when they have been selfish, or when their hearts are heavy with fear or despair. Yet though you may not *feel* like a daughter of God, you cannot deny the reality of it. God claims you: "'Fear not, for I have redeemed you; I have summoned you by name; you are mine'" (Is. 43:1). He also says, "You are precious and honored in my sight, and because I love you. . . . Do not be afraid, for I am with you; I will bring . . . my daughters from the ends of the earth—

everyone who is called by my name, whom I created for my glory" (Isaiah 43:4–7). God would go to the ends of the earth to claim you as His daughter, because He loves you. His incredible love holds you as precious and honored.

Uncondemned But Not Innocent

Even if you are a Christian, uncondemned, you still sin from time to time. When I hurt someone, speak angry words, or do something dishonest, I am always surprised. "How could I?" I say to myself. "As much as God has done for me, why do I continue to make mistakes?" God's voice whispers, "Just say it, Edna! Use the S word: *sin*!" I must face my sin and daily ask for God's forgiveness. Knowing I am far from perfect and Jesus demands *all* my life, I must forgive myself, accept His love, and continue to serve Him, renewed daily in His love and light.

Standing in the Middle

You may stand in the middle of war in your neighborhood, fighting in your denomination, or friction in your family. You may stand in the middle of the sandwich generation, with rebellious teenagers on the younger end and aging parents on the older end. You may feel pulled in both directions. Yet the Light of the world calls you, His daughter, to shine as a star, a light to your world. "You are the light of the world" (Matt. 5:14). You stand in the middle, as a sheep among wolves, as a light in the darkness. What an opportunity for His daughter to remain calm and reflect His light in all circumstances!

The Mystery of Transformation: A Light in the Darkness

Without moonlight, on the darkest night of the year, my neighborhood is almost completely black. Yet a small back-porch light in another neighborhood shines across a valley, shedding light onto my street. Even when the wind blows, with tree limbs dancing, the small light continues to shine through the thick darkness. God's care is like that light. A single ray of His goodness can brighten your life in a magnificent way. A soft glimmer from the Light of the world can transform you into a bright reflection of His mysterious love.

How can you apply Philippians 2:15 to your life?

My "wolves":

God's hope:

My decision to be a "star":

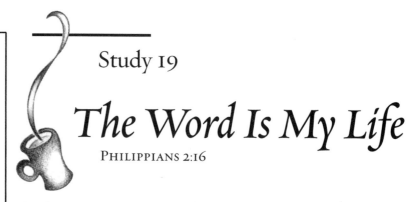

Study 19

The Word Is My Life

PHILIPPIANS 2:16

IN STUDY 18 WE LEARNED HOW TO STAND IN THE MIDDLE OF wolves. Your wolves may be actual wars with weapons. They may be family disputes with cranky children on the one hand and demanding parents on the other. You may face hidden wickedness among your enemies in social settings—even those who call you "friend" to your face. You may fear the unknown. Whatever your wolves, you can depend on Jesus to be there with you in the battle.

I once read "The Interlopers," a short story (by a man who wrote under the pen name of Saki) about a pack of wolves ready to devour a man who hated his neighbor. Since then I have feared wolves. However, just this week, as I prepared Studies 18 and 19, I heard on the radio that no reports exist of a wolf killing a person. Wolves have threatened people, though. As I worked on these two chapters, God spoke to my heart, convincing me that most of our worries never come true. We fear the unknown but with Jesus we can rest, because He knows everything. We can be confident in the face of an uncertain future, because we know the One who holds the future.

Paul reminds us in Philippians 2:15-16 that we live "in the midst of a crooked and perverse nation, among whom ye shine as lights in the world" (KJV). He goes on to say that we are lights because we are "Holding forth the word of life."

What do you think Paul means when he says you "shine as lights in the world; Holding forth the word of life"?

Other translations of "holding forth the word of life" include "holding fast the word of life" (NASB), "hold out the word of life" (NIV), or "as you cling to the Word of Life" (Beck). Williams says, "to hold up the message of life."

> Explain in your own words how you hold "forth the word of life."

What Are Mere Words?

Words are insignificant unless they have meaning. For example, if I said to you, "My dear friend, you are just jikkop!" you would understand that I consider you a cherished friend (words with meaning), but you would not understand "jikkop," because it has no accepted meaning, or message. It's a meaningless set of sounds. In today's world, words hold less meaning than they did in Old Testament times, or even in New Testament times. (Review Study 15 about the significance of the meanings of names.) In my father's day, a man's word was his bond. If someone gave you his or her word, you could depend on it. A person's honor was at stake—something not to take lightly.

Many Christians today still believe in that honored-word principle, but sadly, many others pay no attention to truth or meaning in their words. In some arenas, people admire a person who can fool others by "mincing words." His dishonesty is seen as shrewd advertising, a successful business practice. A few years ago, a television commercial offered a series of musical recordings by the original artists at a ridiculously low price. Later those who ordered the music found it was recorded by an unknown group called "The Original Artists"—not good musicians and not the ones who originally recorded the songs and made them famous.

The Word with a Capital W

You can hardly read Paul's words about "the word of life" without thinking of the Word with a capital W. "In the beginning was the Word, and the Word was with God, and the Word was God. . . . The true light that gives light to every man was coming into the world. . . . The Word became flesh and made his dwelling among us" (John 1:1, 9, 14).

You can hold out the Word of life just as Paul asked the people in the church at Philippi to do. In your own way, tell the message of the Word of life, who gives meaning to everyday lives all around you.

Rejoicing in the Day of Christ

Paul says, "Hold out the word of life—in order that I may boast on the day of Christ that I did not run or labor for nothing" (Phil. 2:16). Paul wants to be able to boast (or rejoice) on the day of Christ. I interpret the day of Christ to be Judgment Day, when we will be

What does it mean to you to give your word?

When was the day of Christ for you? Check all that might apply.

☐ The day I first heard about Jesus. It was a happy day for me.

☐ The day I knew Jesus was my friend.

☐ The day someone shared Jesus with me.

☐ Actually, it wasn't a day; I met Jesus at night.

☐ The day I accepted Jesus as my Savior and knew I would go to heaven.

☐ The day I knew I had a relationship with Jesus.

☐ The day I felt Jesus cared about all my hurts.

☐ The day God saved me from an accident that could have killed me.

☐ The day I knew I could conquer anything, because Jesus helped me face the future.

☐ I haven't reached the day of Christ yet. Explain.

Discuss your answers with your study partner or a friend.

judged for our deeds, or the day when Christ comes to earth again, sometimes called the second coming. Either way, when Paul faces his Lord, he wants to rejoice and not be ashamed of the way he has shared the message of the Word that gives meaning to lives.

Running in Vain

Paul is concerned that he has not run the race in vain. Recently as I sat in an airport, a teenager ran by with large, baggy pants. He held up his pants with one hand and carried two suitcases with the other. His face was red, his hair stood up, and he noisily huffed and puffed as he strode past me. A few moments later, he slunk back down the concourse. His pants drooped, his suitcases dragged on the floor behind him, and his steps were slow. He had missed his plane. All his running was useless. If he had known the plane already departed, he would not have run so hard!

Laboring As I Run

At times all of us labor for nothing—like the deaf woman who vacuumed the whole house only to find she had not turned on the vacuum cleaner. Paul wanted to avoid such a situation, so he asked the Philippians to be true to him, true to Christ, and true to themselves by holding out the living Word to others. God says His Word will not return to Him empty (Isaiah 55:11). If you are faithful to share it, it will accomplish the purpose for which God sent it. You will not labor in vain if you do what God leads you to do.

The Mystery of Transformation: The Word Runs with Me

Instead of saying, "A river runs through it," we can say, "His Word runs through it—my heart." When God's Word runs through you, a transformation takes place: the Word runs with you. The psalmist says, "Thy word is a lamp unto my feet, and a light unto my path" (Psalm 119:105 KJV). With Him inside and beside you, some of the dark mystery is gone. You'll be able to see the path as you run toward the future.

Study 20

Rejoicing with You

PHILIPPIANS 2:17

PAUL OFFERS A GREAT GIFT TO HIS FRIENDS: AN UNSELFISH attitude. Even if he suffers, he rejoices in their good times. Picture this: An Old Testament man takes his best lamb, beautiful and unblemished—one that would bring fifteen shekels at the market. He has had a bad year financially, but he takes his best up to the tabernacle and offers it as a sacrifice on the altar. He gives his best fruit of the vine to the priest to pour over the butchered lamb and then prays as he offers the beautiful marinated meat to God. Since he is poor, his sacrifice is extravagant, but his heart is overflowing with joy. He goes home to bread and water but smiles at dinner, knowing his close relationship with God. Paul says, "But even if I am being poured out like a drink offering on the sacrifice and service coming from your faith, I am glad and rejoice with all of you" (Phil. 2:17).

Offered as a Sacrifice

Paul offers the faith of the Philippians as his sacrifice and service to God. Picture this: Paul, also a poor man as he sits in prison, brings the fruit of his labor to the altar at the New Testament temple. He has chosen the solid faith of the Philippians, his choice believers, as his greatest possession to be given as a worthy sacrifice. He also has bread and water for dinner, rejoicing over his relationship with God. Even if he dies in prison because of sharing the gospel, he can rejoice that he has served God well and has seen that same kind of service in the Philippians.

Offered for Others

As I write these words, it is Memorial Day. At church this past Sunday, our pastor asked everyone to stand who had a member of his or her family die in the service of our country. All over the

Why would Paul feel he is being poured out?

☐ He feels sorry for himself in prison.

☐ He wants to set a good example for the people at Philippi.

☐ He sees the "drink offering" as his blood being poured out for them.

☐ He knows his sacrifice is worth it, if only the Philippians will follow Christ.

☐ He feels weak and forgotten.

sanctuary, young and old people stood. We prayed for them, thanking God for their sacrifice on our behalf. They lost their most precious possession. A living member of their family suffered and died for their freedom and mine. Our pastor offered our "grateful appreciation that is beyond words." I could see moist eyes all over the room as we thought about true sacrifices.

Rejoicing in Me

I don't like to be sacrificed or poured out, do you? While leading in prayer one time, I felt God ask me to humble myself and tell a personal story. I hesitated, decided not to do it, and then could not think of anything else to say. I finally obeyed—with a grudge! Later, I looked up in prayer, saying, "Well God, I hope You're satisfied! What good did that do? I don't like obeying! It's too hard to be vulnerable. I hope You don't ever humble me like that again." The next day I learned that God was working out His will for others who were in that gathering. If I had not obeyed and sacrificed my pride, He might not have accomplished His purpose for those who heard me. Today I rejoice in my sacrifice, knowing it was worth it. God has reasons beyond our comprehension.

Rejoicing in You

In 1999 my daughter Patsy called me. She was then in her early 30s, had no children, and had recently undergone a hysterectomy due to tumors. She said her doctor had just discovered new tumors on her liver. Though the other tumors had been benign, a team of doctors examining her this time had ruled out every kind of benign tumor; the only alternative was cancer. She said, "Mom, the doctor says he may have to take one entire lobe of my liver and part of another, but livers grow back." I fought back tears, afraid to break down before her. "Oh, Mom, I've lived a good life. I'm ready to face whatever comes. I want you to know I do not fear death. I am ready to die if that is God's will." She and Tim, her husband, went to the state's best medical university hospital to see which kind of cancerous tumor she had and to determine the best treatment. We waited.

I'll never forget her phone call several days later, when the results came back. "Mom! I can't believe it. I have a rare kind of

Tell your study partner a personal story, then let her tell you one.

tumor that the doctors had not even considered because of impossible odds." Her voice rose higher. "Oh, Mom, it's benign!" By this time we both were crying aloud on the phone. "I can't settle down . . . I'm so happy . . . I'm just giddy!" And her mother was, too! You could have heard my tearful shout of joy—"Thank you, God!"—all the way from my home in Alabama to hers in South Carolina, even without the phone line! I rejoiced with her all that night. The next day my feet hardly touched the floor! She was going to be well; her future looked bright.

Proverbs 31:25 says, "She can laugh at the days to come." Though Patsy is going through a healthy period of her life in which she can rejoice daily, it's not so easy to rejoice when you hurt or feel the effects of growing old. One of my friends (who always says she is ten years younger than she is) told me of an embarrassing time when her grandson said, "Nana uses Oil of Delay." Paul says he rejoices with the Philippians in their good lives, regardless of his circumstances. You can also rejoice, regardless of your age, your health, or your circumstances.

The Mystery of Transformation:
Rejoicing Brings Peace Without Perfection

So you don't have it all together. You don't like to be poured out. Your life, like mine, is never the way you planned it. You may hurt today. Be assured that rejoicing in Jesus brings peace despite the sorrow, the suffering, and the pain. I refuse to concentrate on what's wrong with my life. Today I rejoice with three of my dear friends, Ann Fuller, Nell Haggert, and Cathy Browne—as well as Patsy—all of whom have offered their faith and their service as a sacrifice to Him.

Friend to Friend

Name some friends with whom you can rejoice.

Unit 5:

Lord, *I'm Living in a World of Imperfect People*

■ ■ ■ As you walk the Christian life,

you must travel with friends. Some are delightful, but some may drive you to distraction. (Remember, we need to be honest. Get real.) You may have unrealistic expectations of them or think they should be perfect—even if you're not. Never fear; God has an answer. Like Timothy and Epaphroditus, you can overcome homesickness and anxiety about your situation and you can encourage others, as these two did for Paul.

A godly woman can
                walk with the alligators
with peace on the inside,
                looking at her needs and wants realistically.

As you turn this page and go for it, ask God to show you how to protect yourself on the journey, to forget the past, and to know the power of His resurrection. Shine like a star! Bask in His words as you study.

Study 21

Seek the Rejoicer

PHILIPPIANS 2:18

PAUL SAYS HE REJOICES IN THE FAITH AND SERVICE OF THE Philippians. Then he turns the tables on them by asking them to rejoice with him: "So you too should be glad and rejoice with me" (Phil. 2:18). If you find it hard to rejoice with others when they are in days of physical and spiritual prosperity, seek the Great Rejoicer. The psalmist says this to God: "But may all who seek you rejoice and be glad in you; may those who love your salvation always say, 'Let God be exalted!'" (Psalm 70:4). God says, "'Then you will call upon me and come and pray to me, and I will listen to you. You will seek me and find me when you seek me with all your heart'" (Jeremiah 29:12–13).

Be Alert

How do you focus your heart totally on God the Rejoicer? First, be alert at all times. The mind wanders even when the spirit wants to focus on God. How often does your mind wander when you pray or listen to a sermon? You've probably heard the joke about the man who sought God's will and went to church, where he heard the pastor say, "Judas went out and hanged himself." He repeated this to himself for a few minutes and then his mind wandered. When he finally paid attention again, the pastor said, "Go thou and do likewise." It's kind of important to stay alert!

Look again at Psalm 70:4 and Jeremiah 29:12–13. Answer the following questions:

Who will rejoice and be glad in God?

1.

Who will say, "Let God be exalted!"?

2.

What two things can you do to ensure that God listens?

3.

4.

How will you seek God?

5.

Beside each of these answers, write your commitment to do these five things regularly. Discuss this with your study partner or a Christian friend.

Be Wise

Committing to 1) seek God, 2) love God's salvation, 3) call upon Him, and 4) pray to Him as you 5) seek Him with all your heart, you become alert and open to His voice every day. Once you are more alert, you must also be wise enough not to follow bad advice. When I was a teenager, I rode in the car with two girls who were bad influences. We drove to a gas station, where the girls proceeded to flirt with the attendant, a friend of my father's. Imagine my embarrassment when they pulled a pornographic magazine from under the seat and showed it to him! I never rode with them again. I recognized early that a Christian could not just be alert to God's voice. She had to be wise enough to obey it.

The Company You Keep

Mary Keith Adair, a church friend, kept me out of trouble as I sought the great Rejoicer. Once we were about to get into a car with a wild crowd when she grabbed me by the collar. "We don't do that," she whispered in my ear. "We don't?" I asked, surprised that she had grabbed me. I was naïve and did not see the danger in that crowd. Later that night, they were arrested for drinking moonshine whiskey. A good friend can keep you rejoicing as you seek the Savior, not weeping because you unwisely stepped into Satan's snare.

Rejoice with Me

Besides being alert, being wise, and keeping the right kind of friends by your side, you need to seek positive experiences. If you

The following may tempt you to avoid God's plea, "Rejoice with me." Check all that apply.

- [ ] Frightening, violent television shows
- [ ] Pornographic magazines, videos, or Internet sites
- [ ] Movies, music, or books about demon possession
- [ ] Anything with unwholesome sexual content
- [ ] A friend who uses foul language or complains constantly
- [ ] Someone who discourages me
- [ ] A person who initiates lust in me

have a choice of watching a frightening mutant monster movie or a Billy Graham crusade on television, which do you choose? God pleads with you, "Rejoice with me" (Phil. 2:18) as you flip the channel to something else.

Let's Celebrate Together

You may also remember certain people, viewing material, or situations that cause your heart to sing. When my sister Phyllis had her first child, she faced a difficult delivery. My father called us periodically to give updates. Finally, he called and said she had given birth to a baby boy, but Phyllis was blind. I rushed to the hospital immediately.

All the way there, I followed a new prayer principle I had discovered: thank God for answers to your prayers, even before you receive them, because faith is the evidence of things you've not yet seen. I began praying in faith, "O God, thank You for restoring Phyllis's sight. I know You have already healed her, and she is well . . . but Lord, I beg You, please heal her." I alternated between thanking and begging, faith and nonfaith.

At the hospital I found Phyllis's husband, Ken, with my father and mother speaking in grave tones outside her room. All three were crying and trembling. The doctor came out of her room, shook his head, and walked on. He had already told my parents and Ken that blindness, a common occurrence following childbirth, could cause permanent mental problems. Phyllis might never come back to us. We prayed. Then I went into the room. Phyllis groped for a glass of water on the nightstand. I said, "Phyllis, here is the water."

Startled, but with eyes wide open, she said. "Oh, Edna, I'm glad you are here! Did they tell you I am blind?"

"Yes." I leaned over and got right in front of her face. "Phyllis, do you know God has already healed you? I have been thanking Him all the way here. You are healed!"

"Oh, Edna," she said. I thought she was going to say, "Don't tell me any of that God stuff. I have been through too much today. I don't want to hear it." Instead she said, "Oh, Edna, I see your face! I see your eyes! Mouth! Nose! Oh, I can see! I see the nightstand! I see the floor! And there's even a dust bunny over there behind the door." I looked, and she was right.

Phyllis's sight returned, stronger every hour. When I left the hospital, Ken, my parents, and I joined in a group hug. We thanked God for her healing. We could hardly contain our joy as we joined shoulder to shoulder, in body and spirit, praising the King of kings. Nothing is better than celebrating God's goodness with family or fellow Christians. My heart still quickens when I remember Phyllis's shining face and her trembling voice saying, "I can see!"

How to Seek the Rejoicer

You can seek the great Rejoicer with Christian family or church family, a mentor, or a friend. You can also encourage yourself, as David did: "But David encouraged himself in the LORD his God" (1 Sam. 30:6 KJV). When every person David knew had left or turned against him—his king, his best friend, his allies, his troops, he encouraged himself as he thought of God's goodness.

The Mystery of Transformation: God's Person Is Already There

Be alert: look around you. The mystery of God's transformation is near you at this very moment. He will not forsake you or leave you without a friend. Commit yourself to be wise. Go to those who trust in God. Find wise counselors and encouragers. Through the mystery of God's Spirit, all these things will transform you.

Study 22

A Letter of Recommendation

PHILIPPIANS 2:19-23

IN THE 1980S MOVIE *THE SECRET OF MY SUCCESS*, MICHAEL J. FOX played a poor college graduate who traveled a long distance seeking a job with his uncle, who managed a large company. After

How can you encourage yourself with God's goodness?

Friend to Friend

Why did Paul send this letter, according to Phil. 2:19-22?

Why did he send Timothy to Philippi?

List traits in Timothy you would like to see in your friends.

reading the letter of recommendation from the young man's parents, the uncle refused to give him a well-paying job. He instead wrote a memo, entitling the young man to a job in the mailroom. Soon the young man realized that a signature on a memo was as good as a letter of recommendation. Starting with an empty office, he requisitioned furniture, a secretary, and a computer. One office at a time, he stepped up from the "shirts" (support staff) to the "suits" (professional staff) and took over the company. A letter of recommendation goes a long way.

Paul's recommendation letter says, "I hope in the Lord Jesus to send Timothy to you soon, that I also may be cheered when I receive news about you. I have no one else like him, who takes a genuine interest in your welfare. For everyone looks out for his own interests, not those of Jesus Christ. But you know that Timothy has proved himself, because as a son with his father he has served with me" (Phil. 2:19–22).

Modern-Day Timothy

Paul sends this letter to the Philippians to tell them that Timothy will visit them soon. Paul sends Timothy so that Timothy can return to him with good news about the Christians in Philippi.

Paul wrote quite a good recommendation for Timothy: He said that Timothy was an encourager. He would bring good news about the Philippians, which would encourage Paul. Paul also said, "I have no one else like him" (Phil. 2:20). He was one of a kind—a genuine, sincere friend. Timothy was more interested in the welfare of others, namely Paul and the Philippians, than he was in his own welfare.

Which negative words from the verses above imply the real reason Timothy was more interested in others than in himself? Explain.

How Are You? Fine, I Trust

I once read a book of letters from George Washington to his mother. He called her Madam and signed his full name at the bottom. Today we are not nearly so formal, yet we still use polite—

but false—terms. For example, we still sign "Sincerely yours" or "Very truly yours" when we write a complaint letter to the bank, though we do not belong to them. We have no desire to be theirs; we just want good service. Yet we might send a personable email that begins, "Hi Mom!" and ends, "Gotta go!" Conversely, in a letter from a vacation resort we might revert to the formal, "Having a good time; wish you were here," or "How are you? Fine, I trust," or "Fine, I hope," though we do not trust or hope anything. These words reflect an expected formal language. Paul does not stand on ceremony with his recommendation of Timothy. He tells the Philippians they can place their trust in him because he has proven himself.

A Like-Minded Woman

Paul also describes Timothy in the King James Version as "likeminded" (Phil. 2:20). Timothy and he agreed on the important things, and he believed the Philippians would also find Timothy like-minded. Paul says, "As a son with his father he has served with me in the work of the gospel" (Phil. 2:22). Like father and son, Paul and Timothy served together, doing God's will. In your spiritual life and in your service, you may find it easier with a friend to walk alongside you, someone like-minded and willing to work with you. You may decide to find a Christian mentor to guide you as you seek wisdom from Christ.

Seeking Christ

In *Seeking Wisdom: Preparing Yourself to Be Mentored,* many women tell stories of what their mentors mean to them. A spiritually older woman to nudge you in the right direction when you have lost your way may be vital to your everyday walk with Christ, but don't forget that Jesus is the best mentor, above all others. Seek Him as the first priority.

The Proof's in the Service

I once met an adorable young woman, Susan Beddingfield, who lingered after a women's meeting. She wanted to go beyond studying God's word, to act on it, teaching her friends a worldview and telescoping her life so others could see the big picture. She said, "If there's ever any way I can help you, please call me."

With your study partner, list two ways you are like-minded.

One day I had a mountain of printing, copying, and stapling to do. I hesitated but then decided to call Susan. Immediately, she went into action. She asked someone to keep her children, came over within an hour, and finished the stacks of paperwork quite efficiently. I know Susan is trustworthy, because the proof is in her service. She came through and "saved my life" when I needed her. Later I discovered that she is a person of great influence in her church and community as well.

I have another beautiful young friend, Tricia Scribner, whom I have mentored for eight years. Seventeen years my junior, she carries my suitcases when we do conferences together. Sometimes she serves me her best "out of the box" pudding. The proof of her sincerity is in her service, but the proof's also in the pudding. Yum!

The Mystery of Transformation: Seeing Through the Eyes of Another

God's letter of recommendation for you is nothing like your picture of yourself. He sees you as pure and innocent, loyal and unselfish. If you have a relationship with Jesus, God sees you as His Son's best friend. You are beautiful in His eyes, because you are a reflection of Jesus. How can that be, when you feel sinful, selfish, and not so pure or innocent? Because He can't see your sin; it's covered by the blood of Jesus, who sacrificed Himself for you. You are also His miracle child, saved by the mystery of His grace, transformed to new life.

A Christian publisher once considered hiring me as an editor for their flagship women's magazine. The personnel manager called their office in my home state but found no one who remembered me. The state office called my church, and my Aunt Alice, who worked as a secretary there, happened to answer the phone. Imagine the wonderful recommendation she gave me! I got the job. When our Brother, Jesus, gives us a letter of recommendation, we are set for life—eternal life with our Father.

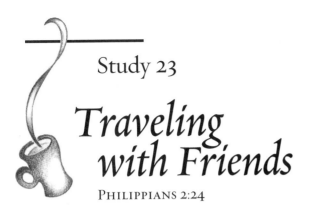

Study 23

Traveling with Friends

PHILIPPIANS 2:24

WHEN OUR FLIGHT WAS CANCELED, TWENTY-TWO WOMEN and I had to spend the night in a strange town. Some of us spent the night in New York, and some stayed in Atlanta. Before this experience we were mere acquaintances who went on a state training trip together. After this adventure, we were forever friends. You probably have a few forever friends, too: the kind that pick up where they left off five years before and talk as if they had never been apart. When these friends and I see each other, we remember things that are funny now but were miserable then. One woman's pillow, which she claimed she could not sleep without, was packed in her luggage and shipped to her home. Another woman turned on the water in the tub and it came out the showerhead, ruining her hairdo she'd paid a fortune to have done by a New York hair designer. She's still screaming about that disaster! A third woman sprained her ankle and had to be taken by wheelchair into the hotel in the middle of the night. Friendships were cemented through adversity. Sometimes when we travel with friends, facing hard times helps us to see who our real friends are.

In Study 22, we read the letter of recommendation Paul sent the Philippians on Timothy's behalf. Paul and Timothy were forever friends. Timothy had stood by Paul through serious adversity. Paul had been arrested in Jerusalem and eventually ended up in a Roman prison, yet Timothy had been by his side much of the time. In this chapter we will see Paul's confidence that he would soon be freed. He tells the Philippians that he is sending Timothy to visit them, and then he says, "And I am confident in the Lord that I myself will come soon" (Phil. 2:24). Perhaps he plans for Timothy to visit Philippi, return to Rome, and then go with Paul to Philippi.

Traveling through the Valleys

A minister once told me in hushed tones outside a hospital door, "We never learn anything in the good times; you know that? God teaches us only through suffering in horrible times." *Yeah, right!* I thought. *How is this pain of watching my suffering child helping me?* His words made me angry. I refused to believe that the suffering we were going through was benefiting me.

Yet as much as I hated to admit it, the minister was right. Through the years, I have realized the value of suffering. I can't remember what God taught me during times of euphoria, but I can vividly remember what He taught me when my back was against the wall, and He seemed to be my only friend. I leaned on the everlasting arms and took refuge under His wing, finding a shelter when I had none.

I have a friend who just lost her father. She took that opportunity to witness to several of her unsaved relatives and led some of them to know Jesus as their Savior. Her dad's funeral was a tender time for those relatives, and they were more open to the gospel than ever before. Just as a death in the family gives a Christian a chance to talk about life after death with unsaved relatives, your suffering gives you the credibility to witness through the suffering.

Paul says, "He comforts us in our trouble; we comfort others with the comfort we received from God" (2 Cor. 1:4). Paul probably could comfort many grieving people in prison. He may have even comforted the guards serving in his area of the prison or families of prisoners. Perhaps he comforted people of political power, such as lawyers visiting their clients under arrest. He hoped also to comfort the Philippians when he saw them. How can you comfort others with the comfort you receive from God?

Traveling Through the Mountains

I listened yesterday as a teenager won a talent contest on television. Instead of thanking the emcee or the judges, she said, "I want to thank my Savior, Jesus Christ, from whom all my help comes." Often I hear winners of athletic competitions or other award winners thank God for His help. What a joy to hear them!

How do you react when you hear someone praise God on national television? (Check all that apply.)

How have you suffered? Describe some times have you traveled through the valleys.

Consider how you may use those valleys to lead others to know Jesus. (Write whatever comes to mind.)

☐ Sometimes I am embarrassed when I hear Jesus' name.
☐ I think that kind of testimony is insincere.
☐ I beam and rejoice that our Lord is recognized!
☐ Such talk is out of place on television; save it for church.
☐ I wish more people would praise Him, wherever they are.
☐ I resolve to do a better job of giving Him the credit for my life.

As you travel through life, don't forget to praise God when you're on the mountaintops.

Traveling on a Budget

Sometimes our money runs out on a trip. I remember a vacation my family took to Florida, where the expensive prices in resort areas surprised us. After one day it was obvious we had to tighten our budget. Instead of eating in expensive restaurants (our original plan), we ate at fast-food joints. Even today, we laugh about our hot dog tour of Florida. When money, food, or other necessities are sparse, remember that God travels with you to help you make your budget stretch. He also promises that your spiritual budget will never give out.

Traveling in Tandem

Do you remember the song "A Bicycle Built for Two"? When I was seven years old, my Aunt Clara let me ride with her on a bicycle built for two. She called me "Daisy," the name of the girl in the song, and we rode a long way, traveling in tandem. I became tired, but she kept us going until we got home. Jesus also keeps us going until we get home—our real home in heaven. No matter whether we go downhill or uphill, in a valley or on the mountaintop, He is always there, giving us the energy to go on.

Do you have an Aunt Clara who keeps you going from time to time, encouraging you to persevere till the end? How long has it been since you've thanked this person? Pause now and thank God for someone who accompanies you on your spiritual journey.

The Mystery of Transformation: God Provides All Along the Way

The ironic ending to this story is that Paul dies. He placed all confidence in the Lord (Phil. 2:24), and yet he probably never saw

Friend to Friend

If you can remember a time of trouble, describe below how God comforted you.

Because I am grateful for someone with whom I can travel in tandem, I will do the following to encourage that person:

the Philippians again on earth. Paul was grateful that God provided for him all along the way, regardless of the outcome. Instead of shouting, "It's not fair!" he was transformed by the power of God to rejoice even in his suffering and death for the cause of Christ. Through a mystery no mortal understands completely, he was confident that his spirit would be with his friends and he would meet them in heaven, where all Christians, including you, will live eternally.

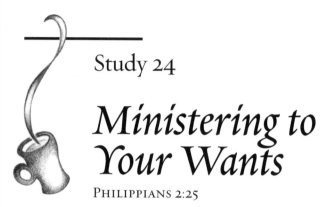

Study 24

Ministering to Your Wants

PHILIPPIANS 2:25

PAUL REMINDED THE PHILIPPIANS OF THEIR FIRST TWO examples of Christian servanthood: Timothy and himself. Now he suggests a third. "I think it is necessary to send back to you Epaphroditus, my brother, fellow worker and fellow soldier, who is also your messenger, whom you sent to take care of my needs" (Phil. 2:25). Epaphroditus actually carried this letter you are studying from Paul to the Philippians. The Philippians sent fellow church member Epaphroditus with money, news, and encouragement for Paul. The Philippians had always been Paul's most faithful supporters. Some time before, when Paul was beginning a church in Thessalonica, the Philippians sent him money. They also sent support to Corinth. After some time, they learned he was in prison in Rome, so they sent Epaphroditus with money again. Epaphroditus had planned to be an advocate, ministering to Paul's needs, but had become sick. Paul felt he needed to go home as soon as possible. The letter of Philippians explains why Epaphroditus was returning unexpectedly.

I Want a Sister

First, Paul describes Epaphroditus as his brother. Regardless of sibling rivalry, usually your brother or sister takes your side in arguments, defends you against the world, or offers you a home when you are homeless.

My friend Theo says, "In the third grade, a large bully named Dutch attacked me at school. My feet flew nine blocks to our house, with Dutch right behind me. I opened the front door of our house and yelled, 'Mama!' Finding no one, I raced down the hall and out the back door—with Dutch reaching for my shirttail! My brother, Thomas, had a part-time job at a grocery store, and I ran toward it as fast as I could. I saw him sweeping the sidewalk in front of the store. I jumped over the broom and hid behind Thomas. He stopped Dutch in his tracks and held him at bay. Dutch started swinging, but Thomas held his forehead, so Dutch's flailing arms couldn't reach him. After Dutch ran out of steam, he muttered and wandered off. Thomas got off work soon, and we walked home, brothers to the end."

Maybe you have no brother, or your brothers and sisters were never close to you. You may need a sense of family or long for an older brother to protect you or an older sister to be your example and confidante. You may feel you need re-parenting, since you had dysfunctional or non-Christian parents who offered no security. Whatever your family need, God can meet it through close friends, brothers and sisters in Christ, or a strong church family.

I Want a Companion

Second, Paul describes Epaphroditus as his fellow worker or companion. Few things are more rewarding than having Christian workers beside you as you do something for your Lord. Working together in church service or on a missions trip, you build a corporate spirit. You may be searching and waiting for a Christian mentor, someone to guide you as you grow in your service. Certainly Paul knew Epaphroditus was such a companion—a resource to him in many ways.

I Want a Soldier

Third, Paul describes Epaphroditus as his fellow soldier. Have you wished for someone to defend you, someone on equal footing who would stand by you in time of trouble?

I Want a Messenger

Fourth, Paul describes Epaphroditus as a messenger. You may seek a message from God, as I do. Many times I have looked at a blank wall above my computer and prayed, "Lord, will you show me the handwriting on the wall, right here in front of me? No one else has to see it, Lord, but I need you to show me. *Show me.*" I asked God to show me His message when my daughter, Patsy, searched for a wedding dress. We began in October, when Tim announced he was giving her a diamond for Christmas. Patsy and I visited an exclusive designer in Birmingham. When the clerk swirled a gorgeous creation before us, I asked the price. His eyes said, "If you have to ask, you can't afford it." His eyes were right; I couldn't afford the price he quoted, over $3,000.

Over the next few months we rifled through dozens of wedding shops from Alabama to South Carolina. We stopped at every mall in Atlanta, Greenville, and Spartanburg, not to mention Pell City, Boaz, Opp, Winder, and Clinton! We prayed for a dress to fit our budget, $500. In February we found the perfect dress in a bridal shop in Mauldin, South Carolina: a V in the front, a bow in the back, and a sweetheart neckline. I could hardly wait to see the price tag: $499.99! Hallelujah! When we reached the desk, it rang up as $350! Hallelujah, Hallelujah! We paid a $50 down payment and ordered the dress in the right size.

I told everyone how good God had been to us. We had asked him for a dress at $500, and He had provided—at a bargain.

At the end of April, my phone rang in Birmingham. Patsy was crying on the other end of the line. "Mom, you won't believe it," she said. "My beautiful dress . . . It's been discontinued. Oh, Mom. What are we going to do? It took five months to find the perfect dress, and we only have six weeks left."

I responded with the platitudes that all Christian mothers use: "Now, Patsy, don't you believe God can do anything?"

"Yes."

"Then we'll pray for another dress. You believe He is capable of providing one, don't you?"

"Yes. (Sniff)"

"Then I'll come next weekend, and we'll find what God has already provided."

"Okay." She hung up.

I put down the receiver and realized even I didn't believe the words I had said to Patsy. I was angry with God, so—since my office had no door—I got down under the desk in my cubicle and shook my fist. "Lord," I said, "how could You do this to me? My baby is crying two states away, and I've left her and all my family to come here to serve You, and now You've let me down."

The next day I got a call from Patsy. "Mom, you won't believe this. They couldn't refund my $50 yesterday, and when I came back today, their seamstress walked in, offered to let out the seams, and the store model now fits me. They are going to clean it and—since it's been discontinued—charge us $250!"

I couldn't apologize in my chair, so I got back under the desk. On my knees I said, "O, Lord, I know better than to act as I did. You have always provided for my needs. You always will. A wedding dress is insignificant compared to You. Thank you, merciful Lord, for forgiving me. Thank you, O my God!"

The Mystery of Transformation: Jesus Is Fullness

Paul says God does "immeasurably more than all we ask or imagine, according to his power that is at work within us" (Eph. 3:20). Jesus is our fullness, fulfilling our needs in abundance! And here is the mystery: "God . . . appointed him [Christ] to be head over everything for the church [that's you and me], which is his body, the fullness of him who fills everything in every way" (Eph. 1:22–23). He is our fullness, and we, along with other Christian brothers and sisters, are His fullness, transformed to serve Him as we live life to the full!

Do you need to ask God for forgiveness for doubting He would provide for your needs? If so, write to Him now.

Study 25

Sick and Tired of Being Sick and Tired

PHILIPPIANS 2:26-30

IN STUDY 24 YOU EXPLORED THE EXAMPLE OF EPAPHRODITUS, Paul's faithful friend. Paul writes the letter of Philippians to explain why his dear friend is returning home suddenly. Epaphroditus needed to recuperate from illness.

When I Am Sick

When you are sick, are you a different person? Most people are. They want to be left alone, or they want constant attention. Picture this scenario: Your husband stays home from work. "Honey, I'm just too sick to go to work. I think it must be the flu. My throat is scratchy, my head aches, I'm nauseous . . . oooh, just let me lie here and die. Don't bring me any breakfast; I'd rather die than taste food. Close the door; I don't even want to smell it."

A few moments later you hear, "Honey, could you step back into the bedroom? You know, now that I think of it, maybe I could eat a little dry toast. It would settle my stomach and make me feel better."

Later, as you bring in the toast, he says, "Thank you, Honey. Now don't worry about me. Go about your business with the children's breakfast."

From the hall, you hear a cheerful voice: "Oh, and Honey, could you bring just a little jam to go with this toast?" The day goes on.

Hand Me My Mood Ring; I'm About to Change

Sometimes we are not ill with a contagious sickness, but we may have a hormonal imbalance. Hormones make us do strange things. PMS, menopause, or other emotional ups and downs may make us sick and tired of being sick and tired. When our moods swing, we can count on God's Spirit to steady us. "I have set the LORD always before me. Because he is at my right hand, I will not be shaken. Therefore my heart is glad and my tongue rejoices; my body also will rest secure" (Ps. 16:8–9).

Prayer lowers your blood pressure, according to *Seeking Wisdom: Preparing Yourself to Be Mentored.* Of course, no one should quit taking a medication the doctor prescribes, but an optimistic attitude and an ability to relax certainly will help our overall physical condition.

What Have You Heard?

In the newsy letter to the Philippians, Paul relates that Epaphroditus knows they heard he was ill: "For he longs for all of you and is distressed because you heard he was ill" (Phil. 2:26). Sometimes we feel better surrounded by our friends. Timothy and Epaphroditus were loyal friends of Paul's who probably encouraged him with Scriptures, testimonies, and perhaps a joke or two. A pleasant word can heal. "Pleasant words are a honeycomb, sweet to the soul and healing to the bones" (Prov. 16:24). As a teenager I heard this false proverb: "Beauty is only skin deep; but ugly goes all the way to the bone!" God says pleasant words go all the way to the bone. Your words make a difference in others' lives. Sticks and stones are not the only things that break your bones; unkind words will hurt you, too. Just as your encouraging words heal others, your discouraging words hurt them.

Spend a quiet moment with God now. Ask Him to remind you of someone you have hurt with your words.

Paul confirms Epaphroditus's condition: "Indeed he was ill, and almost died. But God had mercy on him, and not on him only but also on me, to spare me sorrow upon sorrow" (Phil. 2:27).

Longing for Mama

Sometimes we long for Mama. I believe in the concept of "Mama n'em." This is the idea that when you want to go home, you say you're going home to see Mama n'em. This home is really any place you long for. My mother has gone to be with the Lord, but I still go back to visit my Mama n'em in South Carolina, where I feel a deep sense of community. Some of us can even recall a place of extended family called "the old home place." Family reunions

Friend to Friend

According to Psalm 16:8–9, why will you not be shaken, no matter your mood?

What does your body do when He is close at hand?

Psalm 16:8 says God is "at my right hand." How can you keep Him close?

Write your commitment to make that situation better. I will:

are still held there, and older family members may remember when they lived there with Mama n'em. We long for the comfort of that community.

In truth, our longing is for a greater, better place called heaven. None of us will be totally at home on Earth, because we long to be with our Lord in His perfect home, where He sits on the throne, and the whole place shines with His glory.

Turn Your Eyes Upon the Sister

Part of the perfect community is the companionship of our brothers and sisters as we travel together. Paul knows that his brothers and sisters in the faith will be glad to see Epaphroditus. "I am all the more eager to send him, so that when you see him again you may be glad and I may have less anxiety. Welcome him in the Lord with great joy, and honor men like him, because he almost died for the work of Christ, risking his life to make up for the help you could not give me" (Phil. 2:28–30).

The Mystery of Transformation: Pain Management

Part of pain management is in concentration, not focusing on the pain but on a pleasant or exciting diversion. Part of Paul's pain could be relieved if he knew Epaphroditus was with friends who would be glad to see him. Epaphroditus would recuperate among his Mama n'em—his church family and community. Paul remained calm and confident in Rome as he kept the Holy Spirit in his heart and concentrated on Jesus. Here's the mystery: That same Spirit who transformed Paul can transform you!

Can you identify someone like Epaphroditus in your life—a true friend to the end? Explain why you consider him or her a true friend, servant, and comforter.

Unit 6:

Lord, Help Me See the Truth While I Run this Race

■ ■ ■ AS YOU PREPARE FOR THE NEXT UNIT,
ready yourself for the run:

pick up the pace;
drop those weights of legalism;
put on your running shoes of righteousness;
and look forward through the eyes of faith
to the prize that
waits for you
at the end.

Race day is today. The starting gun is up; all the runners wait at the starting line. Place your hand on the page and get ready to turn it. Ready? Set? Go!

Study 26

Rejoice and Beware

PHILIPPIANS 3:1-2

I REMEMBER THE FIRST TIME I RECOGNIZED EVIL. AT AGE eleven I watched my first television show, called "Danger." In anticipation, I sat thirty minutes before it came on, checking my watch several times. During that episode a woman's husband decided to kill her. When I realized he contemplated murder, I felt sick to my stomach. Facing the reality of evil for the first time, I became physically ill. It took me weeks to get over the vivid images I saw that night.

However, as a child I still had not recognized evil in real life. Most people I knew were Christians, and any meanness they exhibited seemed accidental. As I matured, though, I began to see widespread evil—even in the church. For instance, one woman who came sporadically to the Sunday School class I taught interrupted me any time I began to present the plan of salvation. Frustrated, I confided in a pastor about her and others I perceived on the fringes of our church fellowship. I'll never forget his response: "On the _fringes_? Evil thrives in the _core_ of church fellowships. Evil people manage to get on the deacon or elder boards. They even become Sunday School teachers and pastors!"

Paul addresses the matter of evil in these verses, which include two contrasting themes: rejoicing in the Lord and recognizing evil. The juxtaposition of these contrasts is not accidental. Paul reminds you that even in the face of evil, you can find joy.

Begin with the Joy

Paul begins Philippians 3:1 with a call to rejoice: "Finally, my brothers, rejoice in the Lord!" As you have studied this book, have you paused to rejoice and to worship the Almighty? Pause now and worship Him. Praise Him for the joy that only He can give in the midst of trouble.

Write your praise to Him.

Read the second half of verse 1, circling the words that express the reason Paul has repeated the word "rejoice" in this letter: "It is no trouble for me to write the same things to you again, and it is a safeguard for you" (Phil. 3:1).

Rejoicing dispels fear and sadness. Have you ever needed a reminder or a warning as a safeguard against depression or sin? How does this verse apply to your future?

Friend to Friend

What does "safeguard" mean?

Have you ever had to tell children the same thing, over and over, to protect them from danger? Paul also repeatedly comes back to the theme of joy, the most important treasure in your heart and a safeguard against evil, which only spawns fear and depression. Godly woman, cherish your joy!

Good teachers tell their students what they are going to tell them, then they tell them, and then they tell them what they told them. Paul is following that method: rejoice in the Lord! Rejoice in the Lord! Rejoice in the Lord!

Sending Greetings

Paul says it's no trouble to write. Who do you think penned this letter, as Paul dictated? Check the box that indicates your choice:

☐ Epaphroditus
☐ Timothy
☐ Paul
☐ Someone else

Since Paul was well educated, you'd think he'd write the letter himself. Perhaps he's hindered because he is in prison. Some scholars say he might have had trouble seeing, so he couldn't write well. In his letter to the Galatians, he calls attention to his handwriting as if it were unusual for him to pen his own words, "See what large letters I use as I write to you with my own hand!" (Gal. 6:11). However, in this letter to the Philippians he does not include such a note. We can't be sure if he or a scribe is writing.

Jose, a church member in California, joined others in offering a ministry of penning letters for men in prison, as they dictated the words. After writing a note for Bill, a prisoner who couldn't read or write, he asked, "Do you want me to tell them anything else?"

"Yes," said Bill. He dictated, "And I apologize for this terrible handwriting!"

After Paul reminds the Philippians to rejoice, he warns them against evil that threatens their joy: "Watch out for those dogs, those men who do evil, those mutilators of the flesh" (Phil. 3:2).

Like the Philippians, you may discern evil around you at times. What threatens your peace or safety?

When Paul wrote, the Philippians were new Christians, growing in faith. They also were growing in discernment. As you know God better, you acquire spiritual wisdom and ability to recognize evil.

Pure but Not Naïve

The call to Christianity is a call to purity; God makes that clear. Yet purity does not mean naiveté! Remember, your response, not the situation, determines the reality of the threat. You do not have to be a victim. Also, don't immediately assume those who cause friction are "dogs."

Which of the following tempts you to be sucked into a controversy among the "dogs"?

☐ Someone who seems mean has hurt my best friend.

☐ The pastor acts like a dictator. His secretary said so.

☐ A good woman I know feels as if she is a victim of prejudice.

☐ She said, "I'd like to scratch Vickie's eyes out," and I agreed.

Paul may have referred to Gnostics as "those dogs." They believed that if our nature can be divided into two parts—physical and spiritual—then anything spiritual is good and anything physical is bad. Gnostics showed disdain for the physical by ignoring it. Perhaps you've seen modern mystics who focus only on the spiritual: they never bathe, cut their hair, or dress in fresh clothes. Some sleep on a bed of nails or walk on fire to show they are willing to mutilate themselves as they meditate.

When Paul speaks of flesh mutilation, he may refer also to Jews in his day who insisted on circumcision for new converts to Christianity. Paul believed that circumcision was not necessary for salvation or church membership.

Who are "those dogs" in your life? Paul implies they are Christians' enemies. You may identify people who disagree with you, have previously hurt you, or are "out to get you." Paul says to take his reminder seriously, for our own safety; watch out for those who do evil and/or mutilate the flesh.

Protect Yourself Against Society

Perhaps you've heard this story: A woman entered a clinic with a toe missing. The doctor sewed her wounds, caused by a train running over her as she walked the tracks. The next month she came in again with a hand missing—again a result of jumping from the tracks and not escaping in time. The doctor bandaged her nub but this time gave her a warning: "Woman, you stand in harm's way. Here's a simple solution for your pain: Stay off the railroad track."

The Mystery of Transformation: We See Through Jesus' Eyes

How can you avoid pain caused by evil ones? The secret is in this miracle: you can see the world through Jesus' eyes as He dwells within you. The better you know Him, the better you can see through His eyes the hypocrisy all around you. Your formerly gullible heart can be transformed into a purer heart that is wise and discerning, as you allow Him to rule. You can even rejoice in peace when faced with evil. How? Through the mystery of His presence!

Study 27

The Letter of the Law

PHILIPPIANS 3:3–5

WHEN MY SON WAS ABOUT FOURTEEN, HE ANNOUNCED ONE DAY, "I don't have to obey policemen any more. The Bible says I don't have to live by the law." My husband and I spent the next three days persuading him that "the law" meant the Judaic law, not the law of

Friend to Friend

Check the places you should avoid in the future to stay away from "those dogs" in your life:

- ☐ a bar or club
- ☐ an old boyfriend's or an ex-husband's hangout
- ☐ a gathering place for gossipy friends
- ☐ a place where someone has a bad influence on me
- ☐ an abusive parent's/relative's home
- ☐ a tobacco shop/crack house
- ☐ Other

the policemen in our neighborhood. I then began to search for Scriptures about living by the law, living by the Spirit, walking in the law, and walking in the Spirit.

Call the Law!

In the Old Testament, God made a covenant with Abraham, which became the law for all Jews. "Testament" means "covenant." "This is my covenant with you and your descendants after you, the covenant you are to keep: Every male among you shall be circumcised. You are to undergo circumcision, and it will be the sign of the covenant between you and me. For the generations to come every male among you who is eight days old must be circumcised" (Gen. 17:10–12). Other laws followed, including laws of cleanliness and conduct demonstrating physical, "in-the-flesh," obedience to God. Today, Jewish people still practice the old covenant, circumcising baby boys on the eighth day of life. When Jesus came, He fulfilled the old covenant and initiated a new covenant, or New Testament.

Paul speaks of this new covenant when he says, "For it is we who are the circumcision, we who worship by the Spirit of God, who glory in Christ Jesus, and who put no confidence in the flesh" (Phil. 3:3). Paul indicates that we who believe in Jesus are part of a new covenant of dedication through spiritual submission to Him.

A New Testament Covenant

As Paul renounces any dependence on physical purity as a means for salvation, he gives himself as an example: "Though I myself have reasons for such confidence. If anyone else thinks he has reasons to put confidence in the flesh, I have more: circumcised on the eighth day, of the people of Israel, of the tribe of Benjamin, a Hebrew of Hebrews; in regard to the law, a Pharisee" (Phil. 3:4–5).

Paul's physical vita read like a pedigree: Born into a Hebrew family, he was properly circumcised on the eighth day. Though he was born in Tarsus (giving him Roman citizenship), his family members descended from Benjamin, the favorite child of Jacob (called Israel) and the last child of Rachel, who died giving birth to him. Since Benjamin completed the family of Israel, his descendants were well respected.

Paul went to Jerusalem for his education, where he soon became a learned Pharisee, knowing every jot and tittle (dotted *i* and crossed *t*) of the law. Although he had a right to feel pride in his physical heritage and religious education, he knew these things did not save him. Salvation could come only through Jesus Christ, to whom he submitted as a servant.

Walking in the New Testament

Paul says in another letter, "Walk in the Spirit, and ye shall not fulfill the lust of the flesh" (Gal. 5:16 KJV). You can live in constant contact with Him, walking with Him daily, with such concentration and dedication that you are not tempted to let lust of physical things—even pride in your heritage or in the way you look—overcome you. Paul indicates a new way of thinking: purity comes from within, as the Holy Spirit indwells you.

If you don't need the Old Testament laws, such as circumcision or the Ten Commandments, then why did God give them? I once heard an evangelist say that the younger you are, the more you need physical reminders, but as you mature, you live in the spirit of those laws and do not need to be slaves to them any more. A mother will set up a gate between her toddler and a hot stove, but once the toddler understands that it is hot, he does not touch it even when the barrier is removed. His mother may reinforce with occasional reminders for the child's protection. Spiritual truth follows this same principle: you need to absorb God's words, His disciplines, and His warnings. Once you learn the truth and ask Jesus to come into your heart, you still need reminders of His protection and goodness, as well as your faithful response. You study God's word to learn more about Him, so that you can listen carefully as He nudges you in the right direction. His voice always agrees with His word. God's word is a sweet reminder of the nature of His Spirit, who dwells within.

Paul reminds first-century Christians, as he reminds you, that no intrinsic value exists in the tablets of the Ten Commandments— long since lost—but the Spirit of the Old Testament law remains true. As a teenager, listening to a youth speaker at a chapel service, I was horrified when he threw his Bible on the floor and jumped up and down on it. As our youth group gasped, the speaker explained that the paper pages have no intrinsic power. The Holy Spirit, who makes those words come to life on the page and in your heart, is the instrument of God's power. And as He dwells in you as Spirit, Jesus

Friend to Friend

List things you could brag about in your heritage, family, religious piety, or education.

Now think how you can submit these to Christ, using them to serve Him.

fulfills the Old Testament law, or old covenant, and establishes a new covenant (New Testament) with you.

The Mystery of Transformation: Jesus Fulfilled the Law

I learned a great mystery the day of that chapel service. The spirit of the law is more important than the letter of the law. The powerful Holy Spirit of the Old and New Testaments can make the words of God's law come alive inside you and me. Wow! The living Spirit of God, who dwells within you, can transform your greatest physical sin into purity! I don't know how, but He causes the spiritual to overcome the physical in a miraculous way. What a mystery!

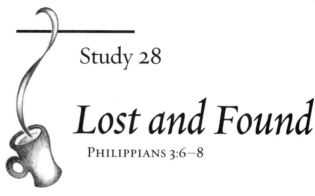

Study 28

Lost and Found

PHILIPPIANS 3:6–8

WHEN I FIRST MARRIED, MY HUSBAND WORKED AS A FIREMAN on the railroad. The company gave every new worker a beautiful, accurate, gold pocket watch, which the workers would pay for in installments taken out of their paychecks. New firemen always worked as extras and could be rolled off a good assignment by others who had seniority. One month my husband had been rolled off every assignment except one, and he knew his paycheck was going to be small. He netted $20 after taxes, and the watch payment of $20 came out of that, leaving him with nothing. He always treasured that watch, because he earned it the hard way.

Years later, he lost the watch and became frantic. We searched everywhere and couldn't find it. I helped him look through all the drawers in the dresser, chest of drawers, and armoire in our bedroom. We even searched through the kitchen cabinets and refrigerator shelves. He had been working on the roof, so we looked outside, all over the roof, in each gutter, and down the drainpipes. Late that night, exhausted from searching, he suggested we pray to find the lost watch and then go to bed. I felt sick to my stomach as we asked God to help us find the watch, which meant so much because of the years of investment in it. A moment later, when my husband took off his overalls, the treasured watch fell out of a long pocket that usually sleeved his hammer.

Paul had once treasured his good deeds as much as my husband treasured his gold watch. Paul had invested his life in physical works to prove his righteousness. After citing his circumcision, Hebrew heritage, and high religious position (see Study 27), he says, "As for zeal, persecuting the church [that is, those upstart new Christians]; as for legalistic righteousness, faultless. But whatever was to my profit I now consider loss for the sake of Christ" (Phil. 3:6–7).

Superwoman Perfect in Zeal

When Paul was still Saul (before he met Jesus on the road to Damascus), religious leaders admired him for his religious zeal in persecuting Christians. I imagine he felt he was perfect in righteousness, since he had memorized and followed every rule in the religious laws. Have you ever felt you earned the title of perfect Christian, wife, or mother? Haven't you at least felt some pride in the hard work you do in the church or in the community? Then you know how Paul felt. He was proud of his religious work. At some time you may have felt proud of your Superwoman image among other Christians, who admire you because of your righteousness. Paul says he is faultless, or blameless. It's comforting to be found blameless. You may have been blamed as a child, and today you try for Superwoman status to avoid blame at any cost. (You may even be proud of your humility.) Performing perfectly as a Sunday School teacher, leader for children's missions or music ministries, or entertainer for various groups at church can bring accolades and affirmation, and these comforting strokes feel good. They bring you a sense of gain or favor.

Circle the things below that bring you a sense of favor among other Christians:

Good Bible teacher
Admired, beautiful woman
"Trophy wife" (your husband is proud to walk beside you)

Discuss with your study partner the things you circle.

Wonderful mother

Righteous single

Neat, clean person

Good cook

Great administrator

Fervent prayer warrior

Witness in the neighborhood/marketplace

Soloist or choir member

Well educated, wealthy benefactor

Other _____

Would you be willing to lose this affirmation by giving these up? Check all that apply.

☐ I'm not willing to lose any of them.
☐ I do not think my motives are impure. I continue to maintain all these because God has called me to gifted service.
☐ I would like to stop maintaining my reputation in some areas.
☐ Let me resign from these! I need a rest.

Paul lost his sight when he first met Christ (Acts 9), and later he lost his status as a Pharisee and his freedom as a Roman citizen. He was financially dependent on other Christians' donations. What would you be willing to lose for the cause of Christ? Are you holding back a few things because you don't want to be seen as a religious fanatic?

 Not only is Paul ready to give up everything for his ministry in Christ but also he is willing to give up everything just to *know* Jesus as his Lord. Even if his sacrifice counts for nothing and no one remembers his work, he is filled with joy because of the privilege of knowing Christ. "What is more, I consider everything a loss compared to the surpassing greatness of knowing Christ Jesus my Lord, for whose sake I have lost all things. I consider them rubbish, that I may gain Christ" (Phil. 3:8).

Good Works Become Filthy Rags

Paul calls all his accolades and accomplishments "loss," "rubbish" (trash), or "dung" (manure). He probably knew well these words from Isaiah 64:6: "All our righteous acts are like filthy rags." The

List things you might lose if you served Christ unconditionally.

Hebrew words for filthy (*ayd*) and rags (*beged*) together mean "menstrual cloths." Imagine the meaning of these words to women of Paul's day, as they realized their virtuous works were no more important to Paul than menstrual cloths—filthy rags, which, like babies' dirty cloth diapers, have to be washed after each use.

Excellent Knowledge: Jesus My Lord

How excellent is your knowledge of Jesus? Check all that apply.

☐ I do not know Him well. I'm learning.

☐ He blesses me with the excellent knowledge of Him through His word.

☐ Jesus is my Lord. That's enough for me.

☐ The older I get, the more I know Him. I never stop learning.

☐ I am grateful for His grace and mercy in my life.

☐ I don't deserve His grace, but He loves me anyway.

☐ My knowledge will never be excellent. *His* excellent knowledge is what counts.

The Mystery of Transformation: I Am the Winner

Today I received an envelope that said, "You are already a winner." I tossed it in the trash bin. I don't believe in getting something for nothing in this world, but listen to this, child of God: in heavenly realms Christ has already paid the price for you to receive salvation. You do nothing for it but accept His free gift and claim the most valuable prize, eternal life. Good works don't gain you any points, but as you lose faith in them, depending totally on Christ, you win the ultimate prize. How does that paradox work? It is beyond our understanding. In this mysterious process, He transforms you, redeeming you for eternal life.

Friend to Friend

Are you willing to disregard your personal accomplishments just to know Christ? Why or why not?

Study 29

Death Is Deadly

PHILIPPIANS 3:9–11

MY FRIEND BARBARA ASKED ME TO GO TO SAN FRANCISCO with her. She had a free airline ticket but knew no one there. I couldn't go, so I called friends in San Francisco to see if they could be tour guides for a few days. My friends were planning a women's conference and asked Barbara to lead a workshop on witnessing. We arranged for Barbara to speak in exchange for free tour guides.

At the California conference, Barbara began her witnessing workshop with these words: "My father is in hell today because he died without knowing Jesus. I was eight when he died. I wish someone had told him about Jesus." As she completed this shocking introduction, a woman named Jessie at the front began to weep. Barbara continued the workshop but soon realized she might have to stop and minister to this woman. When the woman cried aloud, Barbara gave the others an individual activity and went to the front row to comfort her. Barbara assumed the woman had lost an unsaved loved one, but before she could question Jessie, she asked Barbara, "Did your father die in West Texas?"

"Yes," said Barbara, wondering how Jessie knew.

"Did your father work for Parker Drilling Company?"

"Why yes, he did!" At this point Barbara, whose compassion had led her to help Jessie, realized this conversation was not about Jessie but about her. She was stunned.

"Was he called T. G.?"

"Yes."

"I'm the one who did not witness to him before he died in the gas leak."

The woman continued: "I had planned a way to witness to your father, but the explosion happened before I got the nerve to do it. The day after he died, your mother left for her home state, and I never saw her again. I have prayed for a chance to witness to all of you to be sure that you know Jesus. This meeting has brought closure, giving me great peace of mind. I am weeping for joy. God sent me from Texas—and you from Mississippi—to California to answer my prayers!"

Both women today are dedicated to helping others to know Jesus, so they can be found in Him—on earth and in heaven.

Knowing Him, Found in Him

In Study 28 Paul admitted that his Hebrew heritage, religious zeal, or life of legal righteousness did not count for anything compared to the excellence or "surpassing greatness of knowing Christ Jesus my Lord" (Phil. 3:8). Then he adds that he wants to gain Christ and "be found in him, not having a righteousness of my own that comes from the law, but that which is through faith in Christ—the righteousness that comes from God and is by faith" (Phil. 3:9).

Hebrews 11 is a great chapter on faith. It says, "By faith we understand that the universe was formed at God's command" (Heb. 11:3). After several "by faith" examples, it says, "Without faith it is impossible to please God, because anyone who comes to him must believe that he exists and that he rewards those who earnestly seek him" (Heb. 11:6). Paul earnestly sought God.

Knowing the Power of His Resurrection

Paul says, "I want to know Christ and the power of his resurrection and the fellowship of sharing in his sufferings, becoming like him in his death, and so, somehow, to attain to the resurrection from the dead" (Phil. 3:10–11). Look more closely at Hebrews 11:6. Paul believed the power of Jesus' resurrection rested in the believer's faith. The writer of Hebrews says you can't please God without faith. Then he names two points of faith: You must believe that He exists and that He rewards those who earnestly seek Him (v. 6). You can depend on these promises. Here are some other promises:

"For God so loved the world [that includes you] that he gave his one and only Son [Jesus], that whoever [that includes you] believes in him shall not perish but have eternal life" (John 3:16).

"But now a righteousness from God [a gift for you], apart from law [being good, obeying His laws], has been made known [through

Check the activities below that you consider good ways to seek God:

- [ ] Studying the Bible
- [ ] Praying
- [ ] Hanging out with friends
- [ ] Listening to a Christian mentor
- [ ] Meditating on Scriptures
- [ ] Belonging to a good church
- [ ] Other

How have these things helped you know Christ better?

Jesus], to which the Law and the Prophets [in the Old Testament] testify. This righteousness from God comes through faith in Jesus Christ to all who believe [that includes you]. There is no difference, for all have sinned and fall short of the glory of God [including you], and are justified freely by his grace [His unmerited favor—just for you] through the redemption that came by Christ Jesus" (Rom. 3:21–24).

"But now that you have been set free from sin . . . the benefit you reap leads to holiness [that includes you—holy], and the result is eternal life. For the wages of sin is death, but the gift of God is eternal life in Christ Jesus our Lord" (Rom. 6:22–23).

"If you confess with your mouth, 'Jesus is Lord,' [say that aloud now] and believe in your heart that God raised him from the dead, you will be saved [you can depend on it!]" (Rom. 10:9).

Sharing in His Suffering

I rejoice that God has given me these promises. I don't rejoice over Paul's second idea in Philippians 3:10: "I want to know . . . the fellowship of sharing in his sufferings, becoming like him in his death." None of us wants to suffer. None of us wants to die. Yet each of us has suffered in some way in this life, and all of us will die to earthly life one day. We can face suffering and death when we recognize the reward on the other side, "and so, somehow, to attain to the resurrection from the dead" (Phil. 3:11). For this reason he wants to share in Jesus' suffering and death. He wants to be so close to Jesus—to know Him so well—that he will follow Him anywhere, no matter the cost.

Seeking the Power of His Resurrection

Some people say, "I hope I will go to heaven," or "Maybe God will let me go to heaven, if I've been good enough. I hope so." These are wrong responses to a loving Savior, who wants you to be absolutely sure. Review John's words: "I write these things to you who believe in the name of the Son of God so that you may know that you have eternal life" (1 John 5:13). You can know for sure that you will live forever in God's presence.

Check the statements that reflect your feelings about eternal life.

☐ It's simple. I'm good. I'm going to heaven.

☐ I hope I will go to heaven. There's no way to be sure.

☐ I hope my good deeds outweigh the bad ones.

☐ My hope in heaven is sure in Jesus Christ.

The Mystery of Transformation: Jesus' Power Is Within My Grasp

You can grasp the power of Jesus, demonstrated by His resurrection. He was the first in your adopted family to go to heaven. As His spiritual sister, you can follow Him. Because He lives, you have hope in the future. You can be resurrected, as He was; this amazing mystery is not hidden from you. You can know for sure where you are going. Holding His hand, you will not die but be miraculously transformed into a heavenly being to live forever!

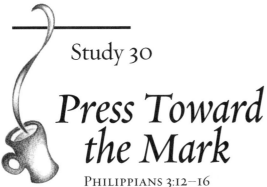

Study 30

Press Toward the Mark

PHILIPPIANS 3:12–16

I FOUND "PAT" IN HER CAR, CRYING. "CAN I HELP?" I ASKED. Pat said she had read Philippians 3 that morning, but she knew she couldn't go to heaven because of past sin. She had an affair with a married man, had an abortion, and slept with many other men. "I can't even confess all of them, because I don't know their names—can't even count them!"

Pat faced a challenge you may be facing: your failures seem so bad that you can't believe God could forgive you. Though you live a respectable life now, your past still may haunt you.

Defeated Before You Begin the Race

If you look backward as you run, you'll never gain the prize as God intended because you are not focusing on the goal ahead. Paul says, "Not that I have already obtained all this, or have already been made perfect, but I press on to take hold of that for which Christ Jesus took hold of me" (Phil. 3:12). William F. Beck translates this verse as, "I don't mean I have already reached this or am already at the goal, but I eagerly go after it to make it mine because Christ Jesus made me His own."

Does Paul say he has already obtained perfection?
☐ Yes ☐ No

Why does he eagerly go after the goal?

Paul is grateful that Jesus loved him enough to die for him. His struggle to be true to Christ is the result, not the cause, of his salvation. As a Christian, you will live a righteous life out of a faithful heart, not out of your efforts to earn your way into heaven. For that reason, you keep your eyes on Jesus and His sacrifice.

Keeping your eyes on Jesus is easier said than done. Despite your resolve, you may slip into old habits. At the least, you may still think about them. Though you know you shouldn't, you may let memories of the past destroy your confidence in the future. God never intends that kind of double-mindedness. He wants no cross-eyed vision; He wants you to focus both eyes on Him and the bright future He desires for you.

Be Ye Perfect? Fat Chance!

Jesus said, "Be ye therefore perfect, even as your Father which is in heaven is perfect" (Matt. 5:48 KJV). What an impossibility! . . . Wait a minute! If Jesus knew we couldn't be perfect (and He did know), then why did He command it? He explains: "'It is not the healthy who need a doctor, but the sick. But go and learn what this means: "I desire mercy, not sacrifice." For I have not come to call the righteous, but sinners'" (Matt 9:12–13). God wants us to admit we are not perfect and answer His call. We are sinners and need mercy. Below are three essential steps to running the race Paul describes:

Which step is easiest for you?

Why?

READY: Face your inadequacy to save yourself through perfect obedience to the law.
SET: Ask Jesus into your heart, to help you daily run the race.
GO!: Forget the past and run the race into the future.

You may want to say this statement each morning as you run the race for eternal life:

I know I am loved today; Jesus loves me unconditionally. There is no condemnation, or shame, in Christ. Since I believe in Jesus as my Savior, I have the free gift of eternal life, the prize of heaven, and the victory over death and sin. I know He has forgotten my sin and wants me to forget. I will forget it. Thank You, Lord, for a good day of freedom. Help me to stay on the path as I run the race with You!

Friend to Friend

The One Thing

Paul says, "Brothers (or "My friends," CEV), I do not consider myself yet to have taken hold of it. But one thing I do: Forgetting what is behind and straining toward what is ahead, I press on toward the goal to win the prize for which God has called me heavenward in Christ Jesus" (Phil. 3:13–14).

In two or three words, describe the "one thing" Paul speaks of in Phil. 3:13–14.

Paul identifies with us who are not perfect yet, but he says he does one thing right. The psalmist also speaks of this: "One thing I ask of the LORD, this is what I seek: that I may dwell in the house of the LORD all the days of my life, to gaze upon the beauty [which means "delightfulness"] of the LORD" (Ps. 27:4).

Luke also speaks of this "one thing" in the story of Mary, who sat at Jesus' feet, worshipping Him. Her sister, Martha, cooked, rattled pans in the hot kitchen, and complained about Mary's laziness. "'Martha, Martha,' the Lord answered, 'you are worried and upset about many things, but only one thing is needed. Mary has chosen what is better, and it will not be taken away from her'" (Luke 10:41–42).

You and I need to focus on the one thing that leads to victory. If you are double-minded, you will be unstable in all you do (James 1:8). You can't run a confident race toward the prize until you do one thing: focus on Jesus.

Forgetting the Past

Once you drop the weight of past sin—excess baggage you've dragged around for years—you will find you can walk faster. Your plodding will become a brisk pace, which will become a trot, then a run, and then a dash of power! The book of Isaiah says you will "mount up with wings as eagles" and run without growing weary (Is. 40:31 KJV).

Pause and share with a friend about a time you soared in your spiritual life.

Paul encourages you to become mature in your faith. Even if you stumble occasionally or look cross-eyed at the goal, God will

List the names of people with whom you could share God's truth.

remind you of the prize. "All of us who are mature should take such a view of things. And if on some point you think differently, that too God will make clear to you. Only let us live up to what we have already attained" (Phil. 3:15–16).

God does not expect to know everything about the journey. He expects you to live up to what you have already attained. In other words, you do not have to be a scholar on every book in the Bible, but you need to live daily by the truth you understand and share it with others who run beside you.

The Bottom Line: Winning or Losing

As you run one day you may have one eye on the past and one eye on the future. On another day you may focus one eye on your family and the other eye on suspicious strangers. On yet another day one eye may focus on perfect Christian models while the other focuses on hypocrites. Don't be discouraged; you are not alone. Run alongside Christians who help you focus on the power you have in Jesus. If you have asked Jesus into your heart, you have already won.

The Mystery of Transformation: You Can Run on Level Ground

Here's a mystery: the ground is always level at the foot of the cross. When you accept Jesus as your Savior, accepting His sacrifice on the cross, you can lay your burdens at His feet. Dear sister, leave them there! When you do, you will experience a great sense of level ground, where the running is easier. You are transformed into a confident, triumphant Christian, who moves closer to Him. Even when you're cross-eyed or looking at distractions out of the corner of your eye, Jesus steadies you and clearly shows you the finish line.

Unit 7:

Lord, *Help Me Run in This Body Till I Get My New One*

■ ■ ■ SOMETIMES YOU WON'T FEEL LIKE RUNNING in your old body, and you may yearn for a new one. In Unit 7 you will learn how to improve your running, even in your old body. You will learn how to recognize body types—yours and that of others. As in previous units, you will see an array of contrasts:

good role models and fallen heroes,
standing firm and running hard (at the same time),
good Christian women who fight,
and physical bodies versus heavenly bodies.

This unit contains ideas about reaching the goal, receiving your reward in heaven, and finding your name written in the Book of Life. So, what do you think? Are you ready for the 100-yard dash? Forget it! This is a marathon. As a godly woman, you need to prepare for the final stretch of the race while you're still in this body. Ready? Turn the page and begin.

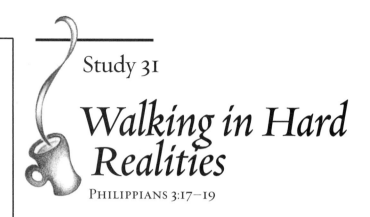

Study 31

Walking in Hard Realities

PHILIPPIANS 3:17–19

MY ALMA MATER, PRESBYTERIAN COLLEGE IN SOUTH CAROLINA, asked me to take part in the processional/installation of a new president at a sister Presbyterian college in Mississippi, where I lived at the time. I said yes, not so much for the privilege of prancing around in my doctoral gown and regalia as for the invitation to a reception at a museum offering a special showing of a Russian exhibition. I enjoyed viewing the Faberge eggs and the furniture of the czars, but I found the president's installation tedious. I stood behind a judge, who said, "I've done these things several times. Just follow me, and you can't go wrong." I turned down the aisles she went down, marched to the music as she marched, stood when she stood, and sat when she sat. As long as I followed her example, I moved in the right direction.

Follow the Role Model

Paul says, "Join with others in following my example, brothers, and take note of those who live according to the pattern we gave you" (Phil. 3:17). Paul knew the Philippians were new Christians who needed a role model. Once Paul was gone, whom did they follow, according to verse 17?

Those who _____ according to the

_____.

Paul and his team had given the Philippians a good pattern to follow. Do you set a pattern of righteousness others can follow?
☐ Yes ☐ No

Why or why not?

Role Models Fall

Paul was a good role model. More than anything else, he wanted to know Jesus. He was willing to follow Him—even to death. However, some role models are not worthy. They crash and burn—sometimes right before the congregation or friends who follow them. Ten years ago the godliest young woman I knew followed her pastor devoutly. She never missed a church activity; she supported her pastor with sacrificial giving and faithful service. Then the pastor left the church under suspicious circumstances. He quit the ministry and denounced Christ. To my surprise, my friend did the same. She quit going to church and began to live an immoral life. Disillusionment over her pastor's behavior destroyed her faith in godly clergy. Her faith seemed to be in her pastor, not in God.

Notice signs of deep emotion when Paul says, "For, as I have often told you before and now say again even with tears, many live as enemies of the cross of Christ" (Phil. 3:18). Would you say that someone who fails as a Christian role model is an enemy of the cross of Christ? ☐ Yes ☐ No

Paul describes enemies of the cross in four ways: "Their destiny is destruction, their god is their stomach, and their glory is in their shame. Their mind is on earthly things" (Phil. 3:19).

1. Their destiny is

2. Their god is

3. Their glory is

4. Their mind is

Look at each of these. I have heard people say, "She is headed for trouble," or "She is hell-bent on destruction." For determined-to-be-bad people such as this, their destiny is destruction. According to Paul, this is a characteristic of an enemy of the cross of Christ. I

Friend to Friend

What happens when your role models fall?

Have you known godly clergy or laity whom you trusted, and yet they failed to be good role models?
☐ Yes ☐ No

How did you handle the situation?

Describe things people do that make them enemies of the cross.

believe Christ's worst enemies pretend to be godly examples and then deceive people in a premeditated scam. They are sneaky and devious, and most of us would agree they deserve severe punishment.

Keep Your Eyes Up

I don't agree, however, that the second characteristic deserves severe punishment. Paul says their God is their stomach, or their appetite (NASB). As I write this study, I have just returned from a church reception where I ate too much: triangular chicken salad sandwiches (you have to eat four to get a whole sandwich), small squares of fudge (they were only a half-inch wide; surely I needed five or six of these), and four varieties of chips and dips (I tried all combinations of the eight kinds, of course). Needless to say, I'd like to forget that gluttony is one of the seven deadly sins in the Bible. It's easy to make your God your stomach. I know from experience.

I can never read this verse without thinking of the Buddha in the local pawn shop with the clock in his stomach. Through this image, Paul may be warning you against navel gazing—becoming too introspective and self-centered to serve others. He might say, "Avoid selfishness and inward thinking. Look up and out, not downcast and self-centered."

The third characteristic of an enemy of the cross is this: "Their glory is in their shame." It's always been hard for me to understand how anyone could find satisfaction and glory in shameful acts. When my husband first told me that people he knew bragged about their immoral sexual prowess, I could not believe it. "No," I said. "They don't tell it, do they? What shame!" It's sad that I no longer innocently believe that bragging of that kind is unusual. I hear of it everywhere, especially in the media. Pride, materialism, lust, and gossip are elements of this characteristic.

The fourth characteristic of enemies of the cross is that "their mind is on earthly things." Walking in the flesh rather than walking in the Spirit is a typical pitfall, because we live on earth. You are surrounded by earthly things: clothes, furniture, new cars, appliances, houses, and entertainment. Your natural self tends to concentrate on material possessions rather than on Christ.

Which of these characteristics most tempts you to become an enemy of the cross?

Followers Can't Walk with Everybody

Paul says, "So I say, live by the Spirit, and you will not gratify the desires of the sinful nature. For the sinful nature desires what is contrary to the Spirit, and the Spirit what is contrary to the sinful nature" (Gal. 5:16–17). If you detect that some of your close friends are enemies of the cross, perhaps they should not be your close friends. If you are a follower of Christ, you can't walk with everybody. Jesus even asked disciples to be discriminating. He advised them to "shake the dust off their feet" (Matt. 10:14) and stay away from certain people.

Join other Christians, friends of the cross, as you stand for Christ and serve Him faithfully. It is vital that you do all you can to walk in the Spirit, not in immorality. Paul says, "If you live according to the sinful nature, you will die; but if by the Spirit you put to death the misdeeds of the body, you will live" (Rom. 8:13).

The Mystery of Transformation: Glory in His Name

It shocks most Christians that people's glory could be in their shame. It is unthinkable for a Christian to brag or rejoice over his or her evil or immorality. Instead of glorying in your shame, glory in His name. The miraculous power in the name of Jesus can give spiritual, physical, and emotional healing. Scriptures record miracles done in His "more excellent name" (Heb. 1:4). You can pray in His name. The mysterious power of the great I AM is still transforming people today.

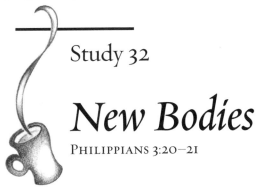

Study 32

New Bodies
PHILIPPIANS 3:20–21

RECENTLY I'VE ENJOYED W. H. SHELDON'S THEORIES OF morphology, with all body types divided into three categories: endomorphs, mesomorphs, and ectomorphs. Endomorphs, with narrow shoulders/broad hips, love interacting with people and enjoy social events. They are usually short, pear-shaped people with round faces. Their most important body layer is inner: the stomach. Endomorphic people love to eat. If you want to please an endomorph, take her to lunch.

The second category, mesomorphs, have broad shoulders/narrow hips. Usually taller than endomorphs, they love athletics. Their most important body layer is in the middle: muscles. They like people somewhat, but they love themselves. Mesomorphic people enjoy exercise and building up their large motor skills. If you want to please a mesomorph, give her a tennis racquet or golf balls.

The third category, ectomorphs, have shoulders and hips of equal width. They are tall, with slender fingers and thin skin that tends toward acne. Intelligent (great researchers and musicians), ectomorphic people don't really like others and require quiet time alone. Their most important body layer is outer: brain/skin. If you want to please an ectomorph, give her a book or a computer program.

We have identified physical body types in this study. Yet, whether you are an endomorph, a mesomorph, or an ectomorph, you can choose spiritually to be part of the Body of Christ.

Conversations in Heaven

A friend told me that since endomorphs love to interact with others, they will enjoy meeting everyone in heaven. (She thinks she and I will be busy making friends and renewing old acquaintances there.) Paul says, "But our citizenship is in heaven. And we eagerly await a Savior from there, the Lord Jesus Christ" (Phil. 3:20). Paul looked forward to meeting his Savior face to face when he got to heaven. Facing death in prison, he knew he might see his Lord soon. Whether we expect to or not, all of us will live eternally, either in heaven or hell.

To claim your citizenship in heaven, what must you do?

Only those who know Christ can eagerly await the Savior. Can you say, as Paul did, that you eagerly await Him?

Citizenship in heaven requires that you worship Christ, the

Lamb of God. Even if you worship Him almost every moment of your life on earth, that worship will not compare to the wonderful worship you will experience someday in heaven. Revelation 4:11–13 says, "I looked and heard the voice of many angels, numbering thousands upon thousands. . . . In a loud voice they sang: 'Worthy is the Lamb [Jesus].' . . . Then I heard every creature in heaven and on earth . . . singing: 'To him who sits on the throne [God] and to the Lamb be praise and honor and glory and power, for ever and ever!'"

Conversations on Earth

If you live in heaven, your conversation will include praise to the Lamb of God: Jesus, who died for your sins. However, you don't have to wait until you get to heaven to reflect Christ. As you live on earth as a Christian, you can praise Him as part of the Body of Christ. "Now you are the body of Christ, and each one of you is a part of it" (1 Cor. 12:27).

As a functioning part of the Body of Christ, you are not alone. Read Paul's words and complete the sentence below. "And he is the head of the body, the church; he is the beginning and the first-born from among the dead, so that in everything he might have the supremacy. For God was pleased to have all his fullness dwell in him." (Col. 1:18–19).

_____ is head of the Body, which is the

_____ .

How much of God's fullness dwelled in Jesus?

To what extent could Jesus claim deity, according to the verse above?

"Fullness" in this verse is the Greek word *pleroma*, which means "filled up." This word carries the sense of having been completed. The next verses in Colossians are incredible. Paul says, "For in Christ all the fullness of the Deity lives in bodily form, and you have

Friend to Friend

Who sings praises to Jesus, according to Revelation 4:11–13?
Everyone in _____ and on _____ .

been given fullness in Christ, who is the head over every power and authority" (Col. 2:9–10).

When you accept Christ as your Savior, you are given fullness; you are complete!

Jesus Subdues All Things in Your Body

Everything you do is under God's control if you are complete in Jesus, "who, by the power that enables him to bring everything under his control" (Phil. 3:21).

If I ever doubted Jesus was in control of all I did, I found assurance when I got a call from a missionary whose daughter had been released from a prison near me. The mother, thousands of miles away, asked me to help her daughter, who needed friends and baby clothes for a two-year-old born in prison. I had no baby clothes and no money to buy a complete layette for the child. I prayed for wisdom. About that time, my phone rang. I answered it, and a young mother on the other end of the line told me about a meeting. I was distracted and apologized, explaining the burden on my heart. After an "I-can't-believe-it" pause, she said, "I am a little frustrated today, too. I tried to exchange new pajamas my three-year-old has outgrown before he wore them, but the store wouldn't take them back. Now I know why! I have the clothes you need, slightly used ones and these new ones, waiting for that precious child!" She later made friends with the released mother, helped her get furniture, donated a car, and enabled a new start in the girl's life.

As the Scriptures say, all things are under His control.

In the verses below, what does God say about how you live?

Do you feel at times as if your life is out of control, or have you trusted Christ to take you under His loving care?

1. "Therefore, I urge you, brothers, in view of God's mercy, to offer your bodies as living sacrifices, holy and pleasing to God—this is your spiritual act of worship. Do not conform any longer to the pattern of this world, but be transformed by the renewing of your mind" (Rom. 12:1–2).

2. "Do you not know that your bodies are members of Christ himself? Shall I then take the members of Christ and unite them with a prostitute? Never!" (1 Cor. 6:15)

3. "Do you not know that your body is a temple of the Holy

Spirit, who is in you, whom you have received from God? . . . Therefore honor God with your body" (1 Cor. 6:19–20).

Right now I pray Paul's words for your commitment to Him: "For this reason I kneel before the Father, from whom his whole family in heaven and on earth derives its name. I pray that out of his glorious riches he may strengthen you with power through his Spirit in your inner being . . . and . . . [that you may] know this love that surpasses knowledge—that you may be filled to the measure of all the fullness of God" (Eph. 3:14–16,19).

The Mystery of Transformation: God Changes Old Bodies into New

Here's the best part of this study for an endomorph such as me: in His own time, Jesus "will transform our lowly bodies so that they will be like his glorious body" (Phil. 3:21). We shall study about our glorious bodies in Study 35. Meanwhile, as I write these words at age 62, I'm looking forward to the body I will have in heaven: no more cellulite, tired muscles, tears, sore joints, or eyes needing glasses. Through a mystery of the ages, we will be transformed!

Study 33

Stand Fast

PHILIPPIANS 4:1

DO YOU SEE AN OXYMORON (A TWO-WORD CONTRAST, SUCH AS hot ice, sad joy, or virgin mother) in the title of this study? A visiting evangelist at our church said that saying, "No, Lord," is an oxymoron, because if Jesus is truly Lord, then we can't say no to Him. We worship and obey Him always. Paul says in Philippians 4:1, "Stand fast in the Lord" (KJV).

Identify what "stand fast" means to you.

Friend to Friend

For numbers 1–3, write a pledge to God, committing your body to Him.

☐ Rise to your feet in a hurry. ("Get up quickly!")
☐ Remain upright, and do not eat for 24 hours.
☐ Hold your ground, firmly fixed where you are.

How can you stand still and go fast at the same time? If you substitute "firm" for "fast," then you can stand fast. Paul warns his fellow Christians in the letter to the Philippians, "Therefore, my brothers, you whom I love and long for, my joy and crown, that is how you should stand firm in the Lord, dear friends!" (Phil. 4:1).

We can stand firm by standing on the Lord's word. When I was a child we sang, "I stand alone on the Word of God, The B-I-B-L-E." As an adult, I sing "Standing on the Promises," which refers to standing on the promises in God's word.

In a California restaurant, I pulled out my last "Thank You" leaflet to leave on the table. The small leaflet thanked the server for good service and offered the plan of salvation in return. For years, wherever I ate, I gave this witnessing leaflet with my tip. As I pulled out this last leaflet in the packet, I wondered if they ever did any good. As far as I knew, no one had ever asked the Lord Jesus into his or her heart because of my leaflets. The more I thought about it, the more convinced I was that they were ineffective. I decided not to buy any more. Though they were inexpensive, I felt I might have wasted the money.

As I looked at my server, a verse came to mind: "Neither cast ye your pearls before swine" (Matt. 7:6 KJV). This waitress was a swine if I ever saw one: spilling food on her shirt; smoking at the kitchen door; flirting with her boyfriend instead of bringing me refills. She never brought me *anything* to drink. Yep. She was definitely a swine. That settled it. I would give her this leaflet and never leave another one. (I figured she could use the tip money to buy a clean shirt.) When I finished my sandwich, I placed a dollar in the leaflet—and then remembering to leave a generous tip as a representative of Christ, I gave her a second dollar. *And that is the end of that,* I said to myself and left the table.

At the cash register, another server rang up the tab. "I saw what you left on the table," she said. "Thank you."

"What?" I asked.

"I'm a Christian," she said, "and whenever someone leaves a witnessing tract, I am able to witness to her. She's [the waitress is] under conviction—I'm sure of it—and I think today's the day she's going to become a Christian!"

Needless to say, I bought a new pack of "Thank You" leaflets the next day.

Oh, yes . . . as I left that restaurant, God reminded me of another verse: "My word . . . shall not return unto me void" (Is. 55:11 KJV). You can stand *on* His word. It is powerful on its own and never returns to God empty. He invites you to join Him as He accomplishes His will through you.

Besides standing on God's word, Scriptures say we should stand firm *in* the grace of Christ. What do the following verses say that we gain when we stand firm?:

_____ 1. "I have written . . . encouraging you and testifying that this is the true grace of God. Stand fast in it" (1 Peter 5:12).

_____ 2. "We have peace with God through our Lord Jesus Christ, through whom we have gained access by faith into this grace in which we now stand" (Rom. 5:1–2).

_____ 3. "It is for freedom that Christ has set us free. Stand firm, then, and do not let yourselves be burdened again by a yoke of slavery" (Gal. 5:1).

When you stand firm *on* God's word, *in* the grace of Christ, *by* faith, you gain encouragement, peace, and freedom from bondage. Each of these is strengthened each time you stand firm.

What if you have moments of weakness? How do you stand then? In the following verses, circle phrases that you believe include the most important words:

"And he will stand, for the Lord is able to make him stand" (Rom. 14:4).

"So do not fear, for I am with you; do not be dismayed, for I am your God. I will strengthen you and help you; I will uphold you with my righteous right hand" (Isaiah. 41:10).

Depend on God to carry you through each crisis—those times you need to stand firm. He will stand beside you. The most important time of standing is found in Romans 14:10,12: "For we will all stand before God's judgment seat . . . So then, each of us will give an account of himself to God." Paul wanted his Christian brothers and sisters to stand when it counted: when they met their Savior in heaven.

Standing Shoulder to Shoulder

You may notice that Paul speaks primarily to his Christian brothers in this verse and his Christian sisters in verse 2, which we will discuss in Study 34. He calls on them to stand in unity, to serve shoulder to shoulder. As we join in His grace, we encourage one another. "As iron sharpens iron, so one man sharpens another" (Prov. 27:17). Paul calls all Christians to stand in God's grace, side by side, serving shoulder to shoulder. It is evident that Paul loves his friends in Philippi and wants them to triumphantly live the Christian life.

Read Philippians 4:1 again, and fill in the blanks: Paul calls them his "brothers," his "dear friends," and his _____ and

_____

This phrase may remind you of your dentist, but the song some people call the dentist hymn, "Crown Him with Many Crowns," did not come from this verse. "Joy and crown" may be translated "pride and joy" (CEV), a phrase we still use today as a term of endearment.

The Mystery of Transformation: God Can Fill Your Sack

An old proverb reads, "An empty sack cannot stand alone." Another proverb reads, "If you don't stand for something, you'll fall for anything." What are you standing for today? If you are filled with the indwelling Christ, standing *on* God's word, *in* the grace of Christ, *by* faith, grounded in Him ("*in* the Lord"), then you can stand as a filled vessel, or sack—sturdy and almost immovable, influencing the world for good. The last part of Phil. 4:1 reminds us, "That [with Jesus bringing everything in your life under His control] is how you should stand firm in the Lord." The Almighty can transform your body, your will, your spirit—everything you are—to be filled with Him.

With or without a partner, decide how you can celebrate today God's power in you.

I/ We can:

Study 34

Two Women Make a Majority

PHILIPPIANS 4:2

ALL OF US HAVE AT OUR BASE A CONTENDING SPIRIT FOR self-preservation. We will do almost anything to stay alive and to have our basic needs met. In fact, we have a basic drive to compete with others, who are also selfishly trying to meet their needs. Even Christians sometimes recognize in themselves an unexpected jealousy and competition against fellow Christians. You and I—and most of the world—will find ourselves fighting against our base nature to keep a selfless attitude.

Life was the same in Paul's day. He singles out Euodia and Syntyche, warning them against selfish bickering. Paul writes, "I plead with Euodia and I plead with Syntyche to agree with each other in the Lord" (Phil. 4:2). Another translation says, "Euodia and Syntyche, you belong to the Lord, so I beg you to stop arguing with each other" (CEV).

When Sisters Fight

Is it sometimes hard to love your sister? She knew you as you grew up. She knows the family secrets. Old hurts may still divide you from your sisters and brothers. Sometimes families do not discuss the problems; the conflict grows and divides the home. The same thing happens in a church. We sometimes do not discuss church problems. Someone got mad at someone else, the church chose sides over the controversy, and they stirred up an evil wind to invade the "sweet, sweet spirit" that fills a community of God.

What is your family's fighting style?

Not Mere Women

One day, while teaching high school English, a ruckus outside my room startled me. As I walked out the classroom door, a coach ran by. The coach and I parted a crowd of students and found two large girls scuffling on the floor. As one of them took a final swing at the other, she slammed into me, shoving me into a combination lock dangling on a locker door. (I had the imprint of that lock on my back for two weeks afterward!) After we stopped the fight and the principal took the two girls to his office, the coach said, "I manage strong football players all day long, but nothing is worse than two girls fighting!"

How about it? Does your church have any warfare among the women? Have you seen women take sides when two of them disagree? Have you ever participated in such warfare, taking sides, gossip, or manipulation?

☐ I have never had a bad thought against anyone.

☐ I admit I silently judged a sister in Christ, but I never said anything.

☐ I honestly must confess I have taken sides from time to time in a controversy.

☐ I have said unkind things about church members.

☐ I have said unkind things to church members.

☐ My church has never had any controversy. We *always* show love for each other.

Church should be the one haven in the community where you can find peace. How can you help your church to be such a haven? (If you do not belong to a church, how can you find one that is a haven of peace, in spite of church members who make human mistakes in their relationships?)

How do people in your church express conflict?

Saints Are Sisters, Too

If a church fellowship is such a great community of faith and a haven of peace, then why do we have so many disagreements? We know we should love each other, but sometimes we find other church members irritating or downright ornery. Churches experience friction because a church is similar to a family; the pastor may call your church a "church family." From Paul's day to this, church families have shared joys and sorrows, money and possessions, and deep relationships. Godly men and women have prayed for one another and shown honest concern, mentoring spiritual children in the church. Through the years, all ages become a close family. As they love each other as brothers and sisters in Christ, you will often see sibling rivalry. Even in a close-knit family of God, watch out for the family fights. Recognizing them for what they are can help prevent them.

As you study God's word in this Bible study, will you sit under God's guiding wings as He teaches you? Ask Him which of your friends—inside or outside the church—He wants you to love in a greater way. Which one would He insist you minister to? Which one would He want you to approach and ask forgiveness of?

Write his or her initials.

Listen to your Lord as He teaches you from Philippians. You will find out more about relationships in upcoming chapters.

Women Empowered

2 Corinthians 6:14 tells one way to avoid gossip, backbiting, and manipulation: "Do not be yoked together with unbelievers. For what do righteousness and wickedness have in common?" Church members may be unbelievers, or as believers, they may let prebelief ideas creep back into their lives.

Paul also says, "For we are the temple of the living God. As God has said: 'I will live with them and walk among them, and I will be their God, and they will be my people'" (2 Cor. 6:16).

Read the two verses below and place a check mark in the margin beside the one that describes you most accurately:

"What causes fights and quarrels among you? Don't they come from your desires that battle within you? You want something but don't get it. . . . You quarrel and fight" (James 4:1–2).

"Submit yourselves, then, to God. Resist the devil, and he will flee from you. Come near to God and he will come near to you. Humble yourselves before the Lord, and he will lift you up" (James 7–8,10).

As you humble yourself, you will step up a level. You will rise to higher maturity as God lifts you up.

Friend to Friend

Pray for the person whose initials you wrote. Then ask God for forgiveness and commit yourself to being a peacemaker in ways He leads you.

State 2 Corinthians 6:14 in your own words, especially as it applies to these problems among your friends.

What Prevents Our Power Turn-On?

I often see Christians who look as if they have hit the "on" button for power. God empowers them to a life of fulfillment and happiness. One thing that keeps us from having that kind of overarching power is our focus on the distractions of a church fellowship: petty arguments, gossip about a "fallen" church member, or controversy over a popular issue. These things take our eyes off Jesus and His joy.

With God in control, you can make a vow of purity as you relate to fellow church members. As you live out that vow, you will resist Satan. Conflict, fighting with a fellow Christian, and silent jealousy in your heart show Satan's power in your life. Satan is happy when he drives a wedge among Christians, but he is defeated when you refuse to participate.

The Mystery of Transformation: God Takes Little and Makes Big

Here is the mystery for today: God can change you (and each of your sister Christians) from people of petty ideas and fighting words to godly Christians focused on big ideas and peaceful words. When you get the little stuff out of the way, God will transform you to do big things. What a change!

Write your commitment to God to stay away from conflict in the church and to be His instrument of peace. Write your promise below to forget petty conflicts and step up to bigger things in God's kingdom.

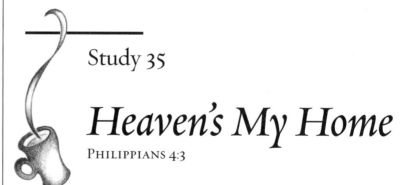

Study 35

Heaven's My Home

PHILIPPIANS 4:3

AFTER URGING EUODIA AND SYNTYCHE TO STOP FIGHTING (Study 34), Paul asked others to help them. "Yes, and I ask you, loyal yokefellow, help these women who have contended at my side in the cause of the gospel, along with Clement and the rest of my fellow workers, whose names are in the book of life" (Phil. 4:3).

What clues does Paul give you in the verse above about the character and needs of Euodia and Syntyche? Check all that are true:
- ☐ 1. They needed the support and help of fellow church members.
- ☐ 2. They had been good workers beside Paul when presenting the gospel.
- ☐ 3. They cooperated and worked well with Clement and others.
- ☐ 4. They were Christians.

You can see number 1 is true: Paul asked a certain person to offer help to these two women. The word for this person is "yokefellow," or *Syzygus* (a person's name, sometimes spelled *Sunzugos*), though several scholars offer different opinions about its meaning. "Euodia" means "prosperous journey," and "Syntyche" means "good luck." Syzygus may have joined Paul as a partner in preaching, just as two oxen become "yokefellows" as they share the yoke and the load of hard work.

Number 2 is also true; as Paul says, Euodia and Syntyche "contended [or strived] at [his] side for the cause of the gospel." They cooperated, working well not only with Paul but also with several others (number 3 above). Eugene Peterson translates the Scripture this way: "These women worked for the Message hand in hand with Clement and me, and with the other veterans—worked as hard as any of us" (Phil. 4:3 *The Message*).

Number 4 is true. When John describes the holy city in heaven, he says, "Only those whose names are written in the Lamb's book of life will be in the city" (Rev. 21:27 CEV). Since Paul makes it clear that the names of Euodia and Syntyche were in the Book of Life, then we know they were Christians.

Guessing about Heaven
Do all these details about the Book of Life and the city in heaven make your head hurt from too much thinking? Unraveling truths about a new heaven, a new earth, and new bodies . . . it's too much to comprehend. Maybe you don't like to think of heaven, because you're afraid of the unknown.

However, I can only think of heaven in a positive way. What a glorious place to go after the death of our earthly lives. I have many relatives and friends there, so I look forward to heaven. If you are a Christian, you need never fear death or what happens afterward.

Who are some of your sisters in Christ that are hard-working and faithful?

How do you view heaven?

☐ I look forward to it.

☐ It's a good place.

☐ I've sinned more than Euodia and Syntyche did. I may not make it to heaven.

☐ Not sure.

☐ Other

Do you need to be a peacemaker in a situation among Christians you know? How can you do that?

Lord, I vow to:

God's word offers assurance and confidence. Remember the verse we studied earlier: "I write these things to you who believe in the name of the Son of God so that you may know that you have eternal life" (1 John 5:13).

Sure of Heaven

You can be absolutely sure of heaven. Joni Erickson Tada has helped take the mystery out of it in her book *Heaven: Your Real Home.* She studied biblical accounts of Jesus appearing to the disciples after His death and resurrection and wondered how, with the doors locked, Jesus could come through the walls. Ordinarily we think of Jesus' body (and ours when we get to heaven) as shadowy and thin. We think Jesus may have melted through that substantial wall into the room with the disciples. But Joni thinks instead that the wall, being temporal (of this world), may be thin, weak matter and that Jesus is a strong, heavenly body of substantial, eternal matter, able to pass through the earthly wall. Just think of it! We will have strong, perfect bodies, able to do many things we can't do on earth!

Help Those Women

Look back at Philippians 4:3. Paul asks others to help these women. We have the same command to help people today. I know a man (let's call him "Joe") who took these words seriously. I watched Joe counsel with a young man, "Tom," in our neighborhood for hours in the yard. Tom's wife told me how much her husband appreciated a good Christian mentor like Joe helping him through marital problems, parenting issues, and questions about heaven. Most of their conversation was not churchy but was practical advice for daily living as a new Christian.

The rest of the story: One day Joe heard that Tom's young son ("Billy") had died in a freak accident at home. Joe stood by Tom during the long days that followed the funeral. Tom visited Joe often, for he had many questions. He couldn't understand how God would allow his son to die. He also felt guilty because he, the only one at home with Billy the day of the accident, felt responsible for Billy's safety. He could imagine Billy saying, "Daddy, where were you when I needed you? I followed in your footsteps every day; I trusted you, but you let me down when I needed you the most!" Those words broke Tom's heart. He told Joe he didn't want to go to heaven, because he couldn't face Billy. He quit going to church and did evil things, hoping God would not allow him into heaven.

Joe assured Tom that no amount of meanness or evil could make God quit loving him. God would never erase Tom's name from the Book of Life. "Their names will not be erased from the book of life, and I will tell my Father and his angels that they are my followers" (Rev. 3:5 CEV). What a wonderful assurance we have that God will never erase our names.

Months after Billy's death, Joe died suddenly. While standing near the funeral tent, Tom felt a comforting pat on his shoulder, which reminded him of Joe's fatherly pat. He turned but saw no one near. Then he heard someone whisper, "You can come on home, Tom. I've straightened out everything with Billy." Tom later told me, "It's a great comfort to know the first thing Joe did in heaven was to find Billy and make things right with him—to let him know his daddy still loves him dearly. I'm ready now, whenever God chooses to take me home!" I saw a tremendous change in Tom. He returned to church, this time with a glowing testimony of God's goodness. Teaching a Sunday School class and other Bible studies, he became a leader in his church. His name was written in the Book of Life all along. God would never let him go.

The Mystery of Transformation: Die to Live

Here's the mysterious paradox: God provides glorious, nonperishable bodies for us in heaven, but we must die to live in those new bodies. We will be transformed from the earthly to the heavenly. We will be resurrected! Paul says, "If by the Spirit you put to death the misdeeds of the body, you will live, because those who are led by the Spirit of God are sons of God. . . . Our present sufferings are not worth comparing with the glory [of heaven]. . . . We wait eagerly for our adoption as sons, the redemption of our bodies" (Rom. 8:13–14,18,23).

Unit 8:

Lord, Keep Me on an Even Keel *(I Have No Rudder)*

■ ■ ■ DO YOU SOMETIMES FEEL YOU ARE STILL IN THE LOW point before the second wind comes? Are you sailing without a rudder, flying without wings? When you feel you have nothing to steady you, trust God to give you joy instead of discouragement, moderation instead of disorder, thanksgiving instead of complaints, and peace of heart instead of worry. Give your heart and mind to hear Him through the words of this unit, and He will show you a glimpse of the future and how you fit into it. Then the last chapter will explain tunnel vision as a way to a wider worldview, as you concentrate on things that are

> true,
> pure,
> right,
> holy,
> friendly,
> proper,
> worthwhile, and
> worthy of praise (Phil. 4:8 CEV).

As an influential, godly woman and one of God's saints, you can do it; don't get bogged down now. Turn the page and begin!

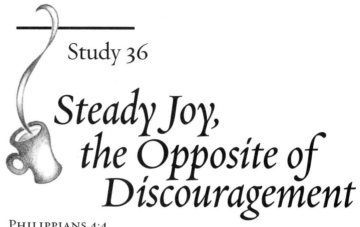

Study 36

Steady Joy, the Opposite of Discouragement

PHILIPPIANS 4:4

JOY IS AN OVERUSED WORD. WE SPEAK OF THE JOY OF COOKING, joy as happiness, joy as gladness, jumping for joy, the joy of camping, or the joy of wedded bliss. According to Webster, "Pleasure" is the general term for any emotion aroused by gratification; "delight" is keen pleasure; "gladness" is happiness, especially as apparent in facial expression or bearing; "joy" is a deep and spiritual experience." Of the four words, *joy* is the most meaningful.

Joy is also a name. My granddaughter is Blakely Joy Ellison; her parents predicted in her name that she would bring the deep, spiritual experience a little child brings. Besides her, I know three women named Joy. One of them, a single woman, recalls often the words in Isaiah 55:12: "Go out with joy and be led forth with peace."

The Bible speaks of true joy. In a search through the Scriptures, I found the word "joy" 164 times—18 times in Philippians. This letter from Paul has brought me great joy over the years; it is the joy book. I recently found the following notes from my study of Philippians in 1966: "Joy! The Christian existence is a life of joy! Steady joy is the opposite of discouragement." These notes are true. If you are discouraged read Philippians over and over; repeat the joy, and "re-joice"! Paul says, "Rejoice in the Lord always. I will say it again: Rejoice!" (Phil. 4:4). Repeat the joy; live in it, and it will seep into your soul, so that you find your heart at rest in the joy that only Christ can give.

Rejoice in the Lord

Look carefully at the Scriptures below and check the ones that apply to you:

☐ 1. "The father of a righteous man has great joy" (Prov. 23:24).

☐ 2. "When the righteous thrive, the people rejoice" (Prov. 29:2).

☐ 3. "The righteous [person] sings and rejoices" (Prov. 29:6 NASB).

☐ 4. "I know that there is nothing better for them than to rejoice and to do good in one's lifetime" (Ecc. 3:12 NASB)

☐ 5. "But be glad and rejoice forever in what I will create, for I will create Jerusalem to be a delight and its people a joy" (Is. 65:18).

☐ 6. "Sing for joy and be glad, O daughter of Zion" (Zeph. 3:14).

☐ 7. "'Shout and be glad, O Daughter of Zion. For I am coming, and I will live among you,' declares the LORD" (Zech. 2:10).

☐ 8. "Blessed are you when men hate you, when they exclude you and insult you and reject your name as evil, because of the Son of Man. Rejoice in that day and leap for joy, because great is your reward in heaven" (Luke 6:22–23).

☐ 9. "You will grieve, but your grief will turn to joy" (John 16:20).

☐ 10. "No one will take away your joy" (John 16:22).

☐ 11. "Because He is at my right hand, I will not be shaken. Therefore my heart is glad and my tongue rejoices; my body also will live in hope" (Acts 2:25–26).

☐ 12. "And we rejoice in the hope of the glory of God" (Rom. 5:2).

☐ 13. "Rejoice with those who rejoice; mourn with those who mourn" (Rom. 12:15).

☐ 14. "Be joyful always" (1 Thes. 5:16).

☐ 15. "Though you do not see him now, you believe in him and are filled with an inexpressible and glorious joy" (1 Peter 1:8).

☐ 16. "My inmost being will rejoice when your lips speak what is right" (Prov. 23:16).

☐ 17. "But rejoice that you participate in the sufferings of Christ, so that you may be overjoyed when his glory is revealed" (1 Peter 4:13).

☐ 18. "Let the wilderness and its cities lift up *their voices*. . . . Let the inhabitants of Sela sing aloud, Let them shout for joy from the tops of the mountains" (Is. 42:11 NASB).

Which of the Scriptures *above* relate to joy in the midst of a crisis?

Which ones relate to joy in suffering?

Share your answers with your study partner.

Which ones refer to joy in singing?

Which ones refer to human relationships that bring you joy?

Which ones refer to your relationship with God?

According to these verses, what causes true joy?

In Revelation, John tells of the ultimate joy. A great multitude of those who worshipped God shouted, "Let us rejoice and be glad and give him glory! For the wedding of the Lamb has come, and his bride has made herself ready" (Rev. 19:7). Jesus, the Lamb, will join his bride, (the Church, those who know Jesus). People such as you and me will be ready to face our Lord; our hope in Him brings the ultimate joy.

Joy on a Timeline

Often you may feel incapable of recognizing joy when you experience it. You realize you have found deep joy only as you look back on your life and see the ways you followed your Lord step by step—even through crises and tragedy. In the space below, draw a timeline of your life, and mark the high spots of joy as you moved from one step to another:

As you look back over your life , consider this: When did your time of greatest joy occur?

Did wealth bring you joy? Why or why not?

Share your timeline with your study partner.

Years:	1–5	6–10	11–14	15–25	26–35

Did relationships bring you joy? Why or why not?

Did the presence of God sustain you and give you joy, even through a period of suffering? Why or why not?

Did you suffer for the cause of Christ? Why or why not?

Do you think you have experienced all the joy possible in your life? Why or why not?

Friend to Friend

As you look back over your life, consider this: When did your time of greatest joy occur?

Alexander Pope said, "Hope springs eternal in the human breast: Man never Is, but always To be blest." Sometimes you do not perceive that God is blessing you, even when you have many things. You may always hope for better days, more comfort, . . . more *joy*. This longing for joy is normal. As long as you live on earth, you will look for a greater joy. Your heart is longing for heaven, when the bride of Christ (that's us!) will be reunited with Him. You can look forward to a time of ultimate peace and joy.

And Again I Say . . .

Listen to Paul's words again: "Rejoice in the Lord always. I will say it again: Rejoice!" (Phil. 4:4). It's as simple as that. Pray this now:

Lord, help me to rejoice in You always—every second of every minute, hour, and day. Regardless of the chaos, pain, and suffering, I will keep my eyes on You, O God. I will focus on Your love, as You bring me ultimate hope, peace, and joy. Keep my heart close to You on earth until I join You in heaven, the place of ultimate joy. Amen.

| 46–55 | 56–65 | 66–75 | 76–85 | 86+ |

The Mystery of Transformation: Supernatural Joy

One of the mysteries of running the race toward the prize of Christ is receiving supernatural joy as you run. Paul says, "But the fruit of the Spirit is love, joy, peace, patience, kindness, goodness, faithfulness, gentleness and self-control. . . . Since we live by the Spirit, let us keep in step with the Spirit" (Gal. 5:22–23,25). As you run over the rough spots, in the mud and dirt—with the Spirit of Christ welling up inside you—He transforms you into a person of glorious joy. In other words, you grin a lot! Go ahead; leap for joy!

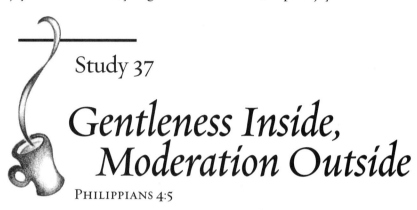

Study 37

Gentleness Inside, Moderation Outside

PHILIPPIANS 4:5

WHEN I WAS A LITTLE GIRL, DURING A FAMILY DRIVE ONE night, I heard a great commotion. I craned my neck to see over the front seat. As usual, my father held the steering wheel. The only problem was that it was not attached to the steering column! Unable to steer, he stopped immediately on the side of the road and said, "Praise the Lord for good brakes!" Many times I've thought of those words and realized how blessed I was to survive such an accident and to have a father who, under pressure, uttered praise to the Lord for good brakes. Some men would have cursed, shouted a few expletives, blamed the car dealer, kicked the tires, or in other ways showed a violent temper. It's easy to be gentle and godly when things are rocking along nicely, but in a crisis a person shows what's inside. My father seemed tough on the outside, but when the chips were down, his gentle heart shined through.

Paul says, "Let your gentleness be evident to all. The Lord is near" (Phil. 4:5).

How do you cultivate a spirit of gentleness? How can you keep from firing hot and then running cold when you face the roller coaster we call life? For me, it's hard! I do well for a while, and then I have a jealous, mean, ornery, angry, or vindictive thought, which will lead to non-Christlike actions if not stopped in its tracks!

A Gentle Spirit

Gentleness is the opposite of violence. On a scale from 1 to 10, with 1 being the most gentle and 10 being the most violent, how you would rate yourself?

1	2	3	4	5	6	7	8	9	10
Gentle									Violent

Describe your violent actions or thoughts.

Describe your gentle actions or thoughts.

For the first question ( ), did you list any of the following?: Rage, foul language, coercion, shouting at your children/spouse, belittling or hurtful words, clamming up instead of talking about problems to solve them, jealous thoughts, or ill will? If you listed any of these, call them what they are: sin. You need forgiveness and cleansing.

For the second question ( ), did you list any of the following?: Seeking peace with someone who did you wrong, touching tenderly (never hitting, pushing, or shoving), speaking softly, showing patience, putting others first, listening carefully and respecting one another's opinions, or encouraging others through kind words.

You may not recognize your violent attitudes or actions. It is easy to fall into bad habits and blame a defective personality or a dysfunctional family for your situation today. (Or blame the other fellow, your closest loved one, or even God for all your misfortune.) If you do recognize creeping violence and lack of civility in your life, you probably don't have a plan for managing your life to avoid violence and build good habits of gentleness.

Share your answers with your study partner.

Look back over your answers. Share with a friend the Scriptures you use to cultivate gentleness. How do you help others (husband, children, etc.) to cultivate gentleness?

If you know you are a gentle person, how is it "evident to all," as Paul says?

Why do you think it is harder to always be gentle with a family member than with strangers or acquaintances?

Check a few ways you have tried to cultivate gentleness.

☐ I choose to live with easygoing people.
☐ I practice the habit of gentleness day by day, before a crisis hits.
☐ I count to ten.
☐ I recite a certain Scripture before I count to ten.
☐ I trust God to keep me gentle and let me live in moderation.
☐ I listen to God and confess when I'm about to show my raging temper.
☐ I choose to speak the truth in love without shouting.
☐ Other

A Bull in a China Shop

Perhaps gentleness is not in your character. Even when you try to be gentle, you can live only so long before you come on like a steamroller. Sometimes you may feel like a bull charging into a china shop, unable to stop your rambunctious nature.

Review these words from 1 Corinthians 13, previously discussed in Study 5:

Love is patient, kind. Love does *not* envy, boast. Love is *not* proud, rude, self-seeking, easily angered (from 1 Corinthians 13:4–5).

The combination of these ideas gives us an understanding of what Paul speaks of as "gentleness," a trait not admired in today's world. In a world of impatient, unkind, boastful, rude, easily angered leaders, we struggle to find persons who are patient, kind, quiet, and gentle in every facet of their lives. This week I've watched on television several game shows that humiliate contestants. Audiences seem to love the insults and outrageous behavior. Do you?

Okay, so we can accept that "gentleness" represents the traits of the word "love" in 1 Corinthians 13 and "moderation" in Philippians 4:5 (KJV). Now, if we could explain "moderation"! How moderate is "moderation"? Where do we draw the line? I see so many gray areas, that I'm not sure, in the heat of battle, whether I will choose wisely toward moderation.

Let's go further in our understanding of this verse (Phil. 4:5). Here's what the King James Version says: "Let your moderation be known unto all men. The Lord *is* at hand." "Moderation" is used instead of "gentleness." Could gentleness be the inner trait that shows itself in a life lived before others in moderation? Gentleness, or a "forbearing *spirit*" (Phil. 4:5 NASB), is a condition of the heart acted out in moderation.

Moderation: Not a Black or White Issue

Some issues are black and white. I know adultery is wrong. Abraham and David knew it, too, but both of them committed adultery when life became gray. The guidelines were muddied just a bit too much, and both of them sinned. Watch out for the gray areas. They are quicksand!

Hold onto the Wonder

When you say yes to Jesus, as He softly urges, you ask Him into your heart to come and live in relationship with you. A gentleness of spirit, or a softness of heart, settles into your heart. As a Christian you will hold onto the wonder of the Prince of Peace, who fills you with awe. The wonder lasts a lifetime. In spite of what the world, your pragmatic mind, and Satan tell you, God will enable you to maintain a life of self-control, moderation, and love, which Paul calls, "the most excellent way" (1 Cor. 12:31).

The Mystery of Transformation: God Changes Gray into White

In an old commercial, people doing laundry worried about "ring around the collar." Actors showed disgust at gray lines inside shirt or blouse collars. Yet, dirty rings inside clothing are common for anyone who works hard—including you. When you are sold out to Jesus, He washes all your gray areas away. He completely cleanses you and transforms you. In His mysterious way, His power erases the dirty areas and washes you as white as snow.

Friend to Friend

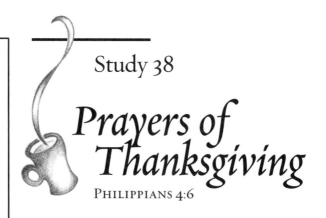

Study 38

Prayers of Thanksgiving

PHILIPPIANS 4:6

ONE OF MY FAVORITE FRIENDS SAID, "I CAN'T STOP WORRYING. Oh, yes, I carry all my worries and cares to the foot of the cross and lay my burden down, but then I pick them all up again and carry them around all day."

In Study 37 we learned about living in moderation, which is easier said than done. The next two studies will help you learn practical ways to build an inner gentleness and live an outer life of moderation. First, Paul says, "Don't worry about anything, but pray about everything. With thankful hearts offer up your prayers and requests to God" (Phil. 4:6 CEV). Establishing a life of gentleness requires that worry diminish. It must! You cannot live in gentleness and moderation and yet distort life through worry. Unconquered worry encourages frantic and rash actions.

Prayer Conquers Worry

When you worry about your life, family, work, or a million other issues, you demonstrate that you don't trust God to take care of you and all these issues. You are saying you do not think He's mighty enough to handle His world. You prove to yourself that you are in control, not Him, and you think you must take care of all concerns.

When you pray, you turn everything over to God. Period. You hold nothing back. As you pray, start with your family and end at the ends of the earth.

For years I have prayed the ACTS formula:

A Adoration: Praise God for who He is. Call as many of His names as you can think of: Lord, Father, Son, Holy Spirit, Prince of Peace, The Almighty, The great I AM, etc.

C Confession: Think of every specific wrong you have done, and ask God to forgive you, because of His deity and majesty and your unworthiness, to save yourself or the rest of the world. Include in your confession all those things you worry about, and give them to God.

T Thanksgiving: Thank God for everything you can remember. Thank Him for allowing you to be born, for your very breath, for a heart that beats, feet that walk, hands that move, etc.

S Supplication: This can include prayer for yourself, your family, your acquaintances, your church concerns, etc. It should also include prayer for those who are ill, for salvation for the lost, and for worldwide breakthroughs of the gospel.

Try writing a short ACTS prayer now.

A doration

C onfession

T hanksgiving

S upplication

Start with Yourself

It's okay to pray for yourself, especially for personal purity, for your safety, and for your life as a Christian to be an example for others. Pray for a closer relationship with Him. It's also good to pray for your children, spouse, or other family members—that God will bless them and guard them against evil or harm.

Don't forget to pray from inward to outward, starting with yourself, family, dear friends, fellow church members, and acquaintances, moving to your local mayor and city council, your state legislators, your governor, and your president (even if some of these are

---

Friend to Friend

Spend time in prayer with your study partner. Using the ACTS model, pray for each other's concerns.

in opposite political parties, pray specifically, fervently, and kindly for them). Continue your outward praying by remembering the leaders of the world, praying specifically for Jesus Christ to be the Lord of all people in all nations. Then sit back and watch the news headlines for God's answers to your prayers.

End with the Ends of the Earth

In 1989, when the Berlin Wall was dismantled piece by piece by common people on both sides, I met with friends that week for our regular prayer meeting. "Can you believe it?" I said. "The Berlin Wall . . . I never thought I'd see it down in my lifetime."

One of my friends, Nell Haggert, said, "Well, I'm not a bit surprised." I turned my head, hardly able to believe my ears. "I've been expecting that for several years now," she said modestly.

"What made you think it?" I asked.

"I've been praying, and God always answers my prayers," she said, matter-of-factly.

Her words changed my life. I had never prayed that the Berlin Wall would come down. I had prayed for my children, my husband, sick friends, neighbors, and my church, but to think of praying for the Berlin Wall . . . well, I had accepted that evil barrier as if I could do nothing about it. I began praying for missionaries, for people caught in natural disasters, and for the latest injustices around the world I read about in the news. I could do something about those situations; I could pray to an Almighty God who was capable of changing everything!

Pray It, Remember it, Journal It

While at a prayer workshop as a teenager, I heard a speaker say, "Whatever your prayer concern is, just pray it, remember it, and then journal it." He taught me how to keep a prayer journal, but I did not become systematic in my prayer journaling until many years later.

Thanks Notebooks: A Family Affair

From time to time when my children were small, we kept a family Thanks Notebook. On one side of each page we recorded things we asked God to do for us, and on the other side of the page we recorded answers. Sometimes we had to search many pages back, because God did not answer on our timetable, but we kept the thank yous going up to God. We never did a marathon notebook, but from time to time we used this method to instill an attitude of thanks and civility in our family. Somehow when we focused on being thankful, the sibling rivalry, spousal control issues, and other family frictions diminished.

Right now, write all the things you can think to praise God for in His nature. Then write things you need to thank Him for. You may run out of room in this book if you thank Him for all He is and all He has done for you, your family, and others. If so, start a thanks notebook in your home.

The Mystery of Transformation: Prayer Breaks Sound Barriers

Have you ever wished you could travel to faraway places? You can, through prayer. Have you ever wished you could change the world in dramatic ways? You can, through prayer! God can dissolve the sound barrier—not to mention the time and distance barriers—as you pray. Isn't that a miracle? Yet, the most mysterious transformation takes place not in the world but in your heart when you pray. God changes you as you praise Him and intercede for others.

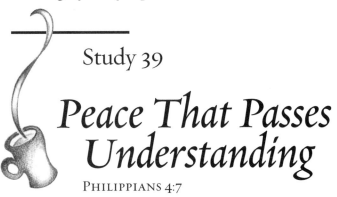

Study 39

Peace That Passes Understanding

PHILIPPIANS 4:7

I SAT ON A MOSQUITO PLANE. YOU KNOW THE TYPE: AN eight-passenger aircraft with fragile wings—paper-thin like a mosquito's wings—and a little prop motor that sounds like a giant mosquito buzz. Before we took off for St. Louis, the co-pilot (no room for a flight attendant) had passed out canned soft drinks, and the passengers were opening them when we ran into rough weather. I

I Praise God For

I Thank God For

Friend to Friend

sat beside a well-dressed young man. When we hit the first bump, his can flew into the air, and cola poured out all over his freshly starched white shirt and Armani pants. He turned as white as the shirt had been! I picked up his can off the floor and gave him my napkin while he tried to mop up the damage. When I offered help, he paid no attention, grabbed his can, and sat in silence for many miles. I turned to read my magazine with rattling eyes as we bumped along. Finally, to my surprise, he said, "How do you remain so calm?"

Without thinking, I said, "I'm not worried. Sometimes I sleep through these bumps."

"Get outta town!" he said. His face was still blanched and stiff.

I tried to remember if I ever had his kind of fear of flying. "The bumps used to bother me, I guess, but now I have realized that the worst that could happen is that the plane goes down and I die. If I die, I go to heaven, and that's better than earth, so what do I have to fear? Once you settle that fear of dying, you can relax and go to sleep as the plane bumps up and down."

"I wish I could settle that in me," he said. The color began to return to his cheeks.

"You can," I said, and I asked him if he wanted to be sure he would go to heaven if he died . . .

God gave me the most exciting moment on that plane. I had the opportunity to explain who Jesus is and that He died so we can be sure we go to heaven. He is the key to getting in! When Christians come to the entrance gate of heaven, they can claim a relationship with Jesus as their Savior. Because Jesus is God's Son, His name is enough to save them, allowing them to enter the presence of a living God.

When we got off the plane that day, the young man looked good. Well, he had a few cola stains on his clothes, but his color was changed on the outside, and his heart was changed on the inside. I have a feeling that today he also can sleep on a plane during a storm.

The ability to relax on a plane is beyond the understanding of one who fears it may drop out of the sky. However, deep relaxation seems natural to one who trusts in the future. Paul says, "And the peace of God, which transcends all understanding, will guard your hearts and your minds in Christ Jesus" (Phil. 4:7). I like these words: "Then, because you belong to Christ Jesus, God will bless you with peace that no one can completely understand. And this peace will control the way you think and feel" (Phil. 4:7 CEV).

Explain what "peace" means to you.

Understanding with My Brain

From the time I was a little girl growing up in a Christian home, I believed in Jesus, a historical figure who lived on earth. In Sunday School I learned that He was born at Year Zero, that is, the years were chronological based on His birth. I was impressed that time itself could be named after anyone. I also learned that He lived thirty-three years, performing miracles, such as healing the sick and bringing dead persons to life. I knew Him empirically, that is, with my brain. I had learned historical facts about this real God-man who lived in the Palestine area. However, the first time I believed in Him in my heart was as a preteen, when I felt His Spirit nudging me. I confessed my sins before an awesome God and asked Him to live in me. From that moment, I *knew* Him, my Savior and Lord.

List things you have learned about God through facts you have read.

Understanding with My Brain and Heart

Empirical ("em-PEER-i-kl") reasoning is the way you think, based on input received through your five senses. For example, you read a book with your eyes and understand the facts you read. Much of empirical reasoning depends on your I.Q. On the other hand, spiritual reasoning is not gained empirically. It has to do with the way you feel more than the way you think; it is holistic, taking your whole self into the spiritual process. It is discernment—spiritual wisdom based on a relationship with your Savior. You read facts in the Bible, but as you meditate on this living Word of God, it becomes real to you on another level. God can speak to you and call to you from His word.

List things you learned about God from listening to Him with your heart.

Gray Areas vs. Gray Matter

A church member said to his pastor, "Brother Joe, I'm afraid today's sermon went right over my head." The pastor answered, "No, Jim, I'm afraid it went right over your heart!" Sometimes you may understand God with your head but not with your heart. Also, at times the gray matter (your brain) may convince your heart to be reasonable, to do the expedient thing in certain gray areas of morality or fear. "Aw, c'mon," it whispers. "Let common sense take over." In Study 37 we discussed that black-and-white issues sometimes appear gray and that it is hard to discern the difference. In attaining perfect peace in your heart, your brain can also whisper, "Think about it. You have reason to worry." So what do you do with the gray areas of doubt and worry that creep from the gray matter in your head down into your heart? Is it really possible not to worry?

Peace in My Heart Without Peace in My Brain

Yes, it is possible to have perfect peace beyond human understanding. When you have a relationship with Jesus, His Spirit calms you in the midst of the storm. You can say, "All right, Lord. I don't understand this. My selfish thoughts tell me to worry about what I can do. Nevertheless, I will trust You, not me. I'll live through this joyfully, and I'll rest at peace in You."

List the things for which you wish you had peace.

Now, pray to the God of peace for peace beyond understanding. Stand on His promise: "Because you belong to Christ Jesus, God will bless you with peace that no one can completely understand" (Phil. 4:7 CEV).

The Mystery of Transformation: the Spirit Transforms the Mind

I don't know how I have been absolutely calm in the midst of crisis, but no one can deny my experience with peace beyond understanding. The Prince of Peace has steadied me through a four-year-old's convulsion, the sudden death of a husband, loss of both parents, a son's near-death automobile accident, and a daughter's life-threatening health problems. Peace? Beats me! I can't understand it. No one else can either. Just accept the transformation!

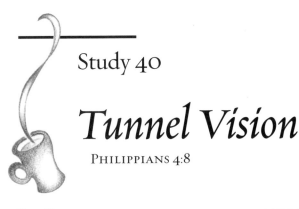

Study 40

Tunnel Vision

PHILIPPIANS 4:8

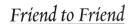
ON DECEMBER 7, 1941, THE DAY OF THE PEARL HARBOR bombing, Uncle John was captured in Japan and remained a prisoner of war during World War II. We asked him how he kept his spirits up during the four years he was there. He lived through beatings, hard work details, and a flu epidemic, in which an American doctor boiled the bones of a mule that had died and gave him the bone marrow to help build his strength to stay alive. Uncle John replied, "I kept my eyes on Jesus. You might say I had tunnel vision; my eyes were fixed on a few Bible verses, and I repeated them over and over."

Paul says, "Finally, my friends, keep your minds on whatever is true, pure, right, holy, friendly, and proper. Don't ever stop thinking about what is truly worthwhile and worthy of praise" (Phil. 4:8).

As you finish this unit on keeping an even keel for your life, remember the pilot of any ship must not be distracted by the heavy waves but must keep his eyes on a mark in the distance, perhaps a lighthouse in daytime and its light at night. One way to stay on an even keel spiritually is to keep your sights on Jesus, the true Light, and press forward toward that mark in the distance, regardless of what others do or what storm rocks your boat. Practice tunnel vision; focus on the Light.

Whatever!

Paul lists eight characteristics, or benchmarks, along the way through your tunnel vision:

1. TRUE—One of the most hated human behaviors is lying. Yet each of us has done it. We laugh at verses such as "Liar, Liar, pants on fire, your nose is as long as a telephone wire," but we do not take lying seriously.

Share with your friend one thought for each category, something she can ponder.

Friend to Friend

Choose which of these you think is acceptable:

☐ It was just a little white lie. I hated to hurt her feelings.

☐ I am never blunt or hurtful, even if I have to stretch the truth a little.

☐ I carelessly said yes without thinking, and then I didn't want to stop the conversation and correct it, because it was no big deal.

☐ I just couldn't tell my father the truth. I was scared. Telling him would have made things worse.

☐ I had to save myself from that embarrassing situation. Okay, so I lied.

☐ I didn't exactly lie; I just left out a few details.

☐ If she jumped to the wrong conclusion, is that my fault?

Whether people categorize their words into "little white lies" or "deep dark lies," in Jesus' eyes they are still liars. Paul sets the record straight: keep your mind on what is true.

However, if you are now condemning several liars you know, consider this: people often lie because they are afraid to tell the truth. Have you intimidated anyone so that they are afraid to tell you the truth in love? Paul says to think on these things.

2. PURE—One drop of red food coloring, dropped into clear water, discolors the whole glass of water. So it is with purity, or holiness. Nothing can be 99 percent pure; it is either pure or it isn't. You and I should concentrate on purity, weeding out any impurity that tries to live in our hearts. Since you can't do this on your own, and neither can I, pray that God will wash you—with all your failures and sins—to be 100 percent pure and clean.

3. RIGHT—Paul also encourages you to keep your mind on what is right, or honest. When our family hosted a large bridal shower, we borrowed extra cups from the bank that rented the reception hall. Several of the cups were broken before we opened the box. At eighteen, I would not have paid for the cups, crying, "No fair!" to the bank officials, but my Aunt Alice, older and wiser, said, "Even though we did not break them, we want to set an example of absolute honesty. It's worth the price of several cups to do what is right." As a Christian, you care about your reputation as a

person who does what is right, and your tunnel vision keeps you focused in that direction.

4. HOLY—One side effect of your tunnel vision is a sense of the Holy One. Focusing on things that are true, pure, and right brings a Presence of holiness that settles over your heart and mind. As you become more like God, your behavior begins to reflect holiness, or virtue. Focusing on these things brings a nobility into your life, as you grow closer to your King—not merely the false piety of good works but a genuine change from the inside out.

Jesus was sent as the pure, unblemished Lamb of God to die for your sins. He pointed to the almighty God, the Holy One, the Author of everything right, Creator of everything good. Then He left His Holy Spirit to live within you to help you in each of these areas. Call on Him.

5. FRIENDLY—Well, now, we've gone from the sublime to the ridiculous—from holy to friendly. The first trait seems awesome and the second seems ordinary. Yet most Christians have a winsome nature they didn't have before they became Christians. After her cousin became a Christian, a child in my family said, "He shines from the inside out!" Sometimes Bible scholars also include the trait "lovely" in Paul's list. A radiant Christian is indeed lovely, shining with the glow of Christ. Hundreds of naturally shy Christians have become soul winners, witnessing to strangers on a plane or bus, in the grocery store, or at the beach. You may become what you once called a "religious fanatic" after you practice tunnel vision and seek a deeper walk with your Lord. You may become a friend to the most unlikely ones as you daily take along your greatest Friend, Jesus.

6. PROPER—Did your mother ever say, "If you can't say something nice, don't say anything"? Mine did. She insisted her children be proper. (Of course, we didn't want to be proper, until we were about thirty-five.) In Study 37 we discussed moderation and gentleness of spirit. Other words for proper might include "self-controlled," "gentle," "moderate in behavior," "admirable," "well-reported," or "of good report" (KJV). Everything you do as a Christian should be reportable as good, or proper.

List areas of your life in which you could become more pure, right, or holy.

To whom can you turn to seek help in each area?

7. WORTHWHILE—Today's world appreciates excellence. Studies show that women don't have time for church organizations that waste their time. They expect excellence in all their activities and want every investment of their time to be worthwhile. In the margin you may want to list a few activities you wish to eliminate because they are not *eternally* worthwhile.

8. WORTHY OF PRAISE—Proverbs 31:30 says "Charm is deceptive, and beauty is fleeting; but a woman who fears the Lord is to be praised." Consider whether your life is praiseworthy, not because you yearn for the world's praise but because you want to please your Savior.

When you focus on Jesus and His righteousness, your heart is humbled and changed. Your life becomes worthy of praise.

Whatever!

My daughter-in-law's nephew, Parker Littleton, age seven, came dancing into my kitchen last summer, singing and quoting a verse from Vacation Bible School. When I asked him what it was about, he said Philippians 4:8, rattling off the list above. Instead of the usual sarcastic "Whatever," he said these words with understanding and reverence. These watermarks, or benchmarks, along the way will steady his life for years to come as he becomes a man of God.

The Mystery of Transformation: With Tunnel Vision, You Can See a Wider View

Here's the mystery of tunnel vision. The more you narrow your vision toward Christ, concentrating on these benchmarks along the way, the wider your vision of the world grows. You see humanity in a new and different way, and, no matter what kind of life you have lived before, you are transformed into a new creature with godly vision.

Unit 9:

Lord, I'm Scared to be a Leader

■ ■ ■ ■ NOW, YOU'RE READY FOR THE NEXT-TO-LAST UNIT.
It's a scary one for many people, because as you study these pages, God may call you to be a leader. I believe God calls all of us to be leaders of one kind or another: some quiet servant leaders; some dynamic, choleric leaders; and some determined, careful leaders. Isn't it great that God made us the way we are, and He will give us what we need to lead? As you pursue the ideas in this unit, you may learn how to

     live with your past,

   become a dog or a flea,

catch the butterfly of happiness,

     open the treasure chest to the future,

       and find deep contentment.

     You can't do these things standing still. I challenge you to seize the opportunity to flow with the rising tide. I hope you can believe God's promise that you can do all things through Christ who will strengthen you.

Study 41

Monkey See, Monkey Do

PHILIPPIANS 4:9

THE FIRST DAY I WENT TO WORK AS A WOMEN'S MAGAZINE editor, my supervisor said, "I am very busy today and don't have time to train you. Let's use the dog and flea method."

"What?" I asked.

"You hop on my back and follow me around; as you observe, do what I do."

I stared. "Well, not literally, of course," she said. "Just watch what I do over my shoulder. You know, monkey see, monkey do." Trying not to feel insulted (and not too happy about being a monkey or a flea), I followed her the rest of the day, watching over her shoulder as she worked. Slowly I learned all the tasks of my job, following at her elbow and learning from her.

Paul visited the Philippians several times; we are not sure how many, but we know that he set a good example. Since the gospel was new to them, these Christians needed models for behavior. When a new idea emerges among us, we usually need to see it in action. You will always need models in your Christian life, no matter how long you've been a Christian. You will also serve as a model for others whether you plan it or not.

Paul says to the church members at Philippi, "Whatever you have learned or received or heard from me, or seen in me—put it into practice. And the God of peace will be with you" (Phil. 4:9).

For more about mentoring, study *Woman to Woman: Preparing Yourself to Mentor* and *Seeking Wisdom: Preparing Yourself to Be Mentored,* both by Edna Ellison and Tricia Scribner.

Pause a moment now and thank God for your good examples of faith. You may have had excellent Christian parents or mentors, but nothing can take the place of Jesus as your example.

Name people in your family who are good examples to you of Christian behavior.

1.

2.

3.

4.

Name godly people who have mentored you (guided, encouraged, or taught you).

1.

2.

3.

4.

What You See in God, Do

In the Old Testament, God demonstrated His love to patriarchs such as Abraham, leaders such as Moses, prophets such as Isaiah, judges such as Deborah, and kings such as David. The Old Testament unfolds the story of God's nature, His people, and the way they relate. He sets examples of how people should relate to others. The New Testament tells the story of God's sending His only Son to show us, in flesh and blood, how to relate to Him and to each other. As you read about Jesus, you will find your personal example of how to relate to others in love. As you meditate on His Word, clearer meaning for His example of love and truth will become evident.

What You See in Yourself, Do, Godly Woman!

In 1813 Admiral Oliver Perry sent this message from the USS Niagara to William Henry Harrison: "We have met the enemy, and they are ours." In the twentieth century, the comic strip character Pogo said, "We have met the enemy, and he is us." Sometimes we are our own worst enemies, as Pogo indicates, but most of the time, we Christians have more ability than we realize. Stop for a moment and consider your qualifications as a godly woman with a lot to give to your Lord. "Consider now, for the LORD has chosen you to build a temple as a sanctuary. Be strong and do the work" (1 Chron. 28:10). God will build His church with people such as you, those who have the strength of character and ability to serve.

I have found that most women do not feel qualified to serve Him. First, they feel they are not good enough. They hold on to past sins and never quite shake them, though they have confessed, and God has forgiven them. Second, they feel they have nothing to offer. They fail to see how much they have grown in Christ. It's true that some of them are spiritual babes in Christ; they have not matured in their faith. However, many of them are filled with godly wisdom from years of experience with the Savior. They are so humble that they cannot recognize their beautiful qualifications—the expertise of a mature woman of God! Third, they feel service is too hard for them, even when they have mastered many harder things: managing a house; taking care of a family; working in a variety of jobs; and expending physical, social, intellectual, and psychological energy on the most important relationships in the world.

Friend to Friend

In what ways are you strong? List three:

How about you? Have you ever used these three excuses for not being all God wants you to be? Have you hesitated to step up to a position of leadership because of these three reasons?

I. I'M NOT GOOD ENOUGH. List a few things you have not totally given to God and forgotten. Pray now for His mercy to allow you to forget completely, as He has done. Relinquish the past. Consider the blessings from the Almighty, who empowers you to do greater things for Him.

I'm not good enough.
I.
2.
3.
4.

2. I HAVE NOTHING TO OFFER. While humility is a good trait, don't be too humble to list your good qualities and allow God to show you how He can use them. Offer your strong points of personality, material possessions, and talents to Him now.

I have nothing to offer.
I.
2.
3.
4.

3. SERVING GOD IS TOO HARD FOR ME. God will never ask you to serve Him unless He gives you the gifts to serve. He will never violate you, humiliate you, or ask you to do anything He has not enabled or gifted you to do. Take time now to submit your life, your talents, and your gifts to Him, no matter how hard the task. Then watch for the unbelievable opportunities He presents!

Serving God is too hard for me.
I.
2.
3.
4.

Jesus was a great example to those who lived in His time, and we can still look to Him today, but others need someone like you to lead them into a deeper walk with Him. He may be calling you to lead in some area, small or large. Children, youth, and adults may be pleading, "Lord, I know You are always with me, but I want Jesus with skin on! Send someone to help me today." Look around and watch for the "holy coincidences," when God brings someone into your path or offers you wonderful opportunities to show His love.

In Word and Deed
Colossians 3:17 says, "Whatever you do, whether in word or deed, do it all in the name of the Lord Jesus." Whether you are witnessing to your mother, speaking to a group of children in your church, or leading recreation activities in a poor neighborhood, show God's love in your special way, as God leads.

The Mystery of Transformation: Words Transformed to Deeds

God's process is an ever-changing mystery. As we pray, our hearts begin to form a concept of ministry to others. We think of it; then we say it; then we do it. Begin now with that formula: Pray, Think, Say, Do. Commune with Him until He shows you opportunities. Speak with Him and others about possibilities. Then do whatever He asks. The result will be peace in the doing. Your heart will be transformed from perplexity to peace, from hesitance to helping, from mystery to movement, from shy to shouting! "And the God of peace will be with you" (Phil. 4:9). Amen.

Study 42

Missed Opportunities: Don't Hesitate

PHILIPPIANS 4:10

A YOUNG STUDENT OF MINE, JOEY MCNEILL, FINISHED COLLEGE and seminary and then worked summers at a Christian retreat center at a South Carolina beach near the Grand Strand. One day he was running on the beach, and he heard God speak to him. He stopped running immediately and sat on one of the black jetties jutting out into the water. "Okay, Lord, what do You want to say to me?"

He said he heard God clearly in his mind: "Joey, what do you think of Darlene?" *Darlene.* Joey mulled over her name in his mind. He had not seen her in two years but had been close to her in college. "Well, Lord, I guess I always thought she was the one for me. She is a fine Christian, I enjoyed her company . . . I hadn't thought much about it."

"You think she's a good Christian, the one for you, you say. Isn't it about time you did something about it?"

"Yes, Sir, it is! . . . I do love her—always have. It's about time I did something about it!"

Joey called Darlene that day, proposed to her the next weekend, and married her a few months later. Today Joey and Darlene serve as a team in Virginia. He is pastor of a growing church, and Darlene works with learning disabled readers in their community. Their strong marriage, their two teenaged children, and their successful service for God in their town are the result of Joey's taking the opportunity God offered him.

Shakespeare said,
"There is a tide in the affairs of men
Which, taken at the flood, leads on to fortune;
Omitted, all the voyage of their life
Is bound in shallows and in miseries."
(*Julius Caesar*, IV, ii)

Is God saying something to you at this moment? Shakespeare said we need to take the opportunity presented to us. When the tide comes in, we need to sail! It may never be quite full enough again to support so strong a voyage.

Paul says it this way: "I rejoice greatly in the Lord that at last you have renewed your concern for me. Indeed, you have been concerned, but you had no opportunity to show it" (Phil. 4:10). The Contemporary English Version says, "Actually, you were thinking about me all along, but you didn't have any chance to show it." Paul was grateful for the gifts and care the Philippians had shown him in Rome. He knew they would have done more, but given the distance and communication in those days, they didn't have the opportunity we have today. They had lost touch with him, perhaps wondering if he were still alive. Now he rejoices greatly (there's that theme of joy again) that they have renewed their concern for him.

Living with Regret

Paul speaks in positive terms but hints at the negative. Shakespeare presents the negative: If you don't take the opportunity that leads to good things, then "omitted, all the voyages of their life/Is bound in shallows and in miseries." It's easy for anyone to get bound in shallows—that is, stuck in the mud. You can be miserable when you fail to take an opportunity and then regret it the rest of your days. I know many people depressed over the "what ifs" of their lives: What if I'd taken that job? What if I'd moved out of town when I was twenty-one? What if my mother had not died? What if . . .

Lacking Opportunity

Like the Philippians, have "you had no opportunity to show it"? That is, your talent? Your love? Your leadership ability? What do you wish you had an opportunity to show, but the opportunity has never come?

How do you feel about that lack of opportunity?

What could you do about the opportunity now?

Living with the Past

Alfred Lord Tennyson wrote about Ulysses wasting "idle tears," thinking about the past. You may have cried idle tears, not only over the missed opportunities but also over other regrets in your past. Perhaps you regret things you did, not things you wish you had done.

You may decide you spend too much time regretting things in your past; you have not made peace with those who hurt you. If so, you may want to seek counseling, talk to your prayer partner, or find a twelve-step program in your community or through your church, helping you forgive. As you seek help, do not despair. God loves you and cares about these deep hurts. You can have hope in Him!

Friend to Friend

List a few of your "what ifs."

What regrets do you have from your past?

How could things have been different?

What can you do about it now?

No Jesus, No Power/Know Jesus, Know Power

The Bible has much to say about opportunities. In the famous "By faith" chapter, the writer of Hebrews 11 lists many people who took advantage of the opportunities before them, because they lived by faith. Abraham moved hundreds of miles to claim the opportunity and promise God had for him. (For a complete list of all these faith heroes/heroines, read Hebrews 11:1–34.) "All these people were still living by faith when they died. . . . If they had been thinking of the country they had left, they would have had opportunity to return. Instead, they were longing for a better country—a heavenly one. Therefore God is not ashamed to be called their God, for he has prepared a city for them" (Heb. 11:13,15–16).

• In the Scripture above, how were these people living when they died? By _____.

• What would God have given them if they had looked back at the past? _____

• They would have had _____ to _____.

• Instead, these people of faith were longing for a _____ country, a _____ one.

• How did God reward them for living by faith?

When you have Jesus in your heart, you have the power of His Holy Spirit. Through faith in Him—as you grow in Him and know Him—you will find unbelievable courage and power to serve Him.

Take the Tide, Flourish Again

Because God allows you to choose, you can look back and dwell in the past (the country you had left). Yet, as a person of faith, you will look to the future. Trust God for the courage to take the opportunities

He gives you. Paul says, "Therefore, as we have opportunity, let us do good to all people." (Gal. 6:10). Hungry people need food, sick people need nursing care, hurting people need a kind touch, and sad people need encouragement. What do you have to give?

Circle the things you can do: smile, work at a shelter, pray, send a note, email someone, read a story, teach someone to read, write a letter for someone who can't write, sit by a sickbed, talk to an unlovely person, read the Bible to someone, volunteer, type, cook, sew, call, provide lights, provide a home, provide transportation, give money, baby-sit, give time, sing, play a musical instrument, grow flowers, share food, teach, tell jokes, play games, guide, counsel, listen, perform drama, other_____.

Jesus said, "'No one who puts his hand to the plow and looks back is fit for service in the kingdom of God'" (Luke 9:62). My grandmother always said, "Time and tide wait for no man." Take the tide! Seize the day! Bloom where you're planted. Whatever cliché you use to describe it, use the moments you have before they are gone. Do not hesitate or waste time; do whatever God gives you opportunity to do, in faith—now!

The Mystery of Transformation: No Past, Present, or Future?

A professor showed our class we had no past, present, or future. First, he asked, "Where's the past?" We admitted it was gone. "Where's the future?" We admitted it was gone, too, at least for the moment; it didn't exist yet. "Then," he said, "show me the present." We said, "Now," but he proved to us that by the time we said, "Now," the present was already gone—it was already passed and past. Now, here's the mystery: the past is gone. Forget it! The present is gone by the time you recognize it. However, God transforms the future as you look toward it. Take His opportunities. Hallelujah!

Friend to Friend

Share with your friend the answers you circle.

Study 43

To Be Content or Not To Be: That Is The Question

PHILIPPIANS 4:11–12

IN OUR FAMILY WE LAUGH ABOUT THE OLD SAYING, "I DON'T DO windows." (We do, of course, but we're not very good at it. Only my son can clean a window or mirror without leaving streaks.) Yet many people make a good living washing windows. Once a man spoke to our church in South Carolina, telling about opportunities God provides even when we are not content about them. During the Korean War this man wanted to do something noble in the army, yet his outfit always put him to work "policing the area": picking up trash and washing windows. Every day, men would go out on expeditions, leaving him behind to police the area. He got sick and tired of washing windows, a backbreaking chore. While others flew planes and came back as heroes, while others went out on maneuvers and came back decorated with Congressional Medals of Honor, he was busy washing windows. After the war, others got jobs as commercial airline pilots, computer programmers, and leaders of large companies, but he had difficulty finding work. Prospective employers asked, "What did you do in the army?" and he answered, "Washed windows."

Finally, one day, after applying for several jobs, he looked up. All the buildings in the city had windows, hundreds of windows. He went into the window-washing business and quickly became a millionaire. He told us that God has a plan for each of us. We need to be content with whatever He gives us. These things will prepare us and lead us in His plan. But we need to look up to find it.

Wants Versus Needs

If you serve with courage to lead others closer to Him, you may not yet understand His plan. First, consider your needs in your special place of service. Complete the lists in the sidebar.

Now, consider this: did you list air, food, and water—the three most essential elements for life?

Sometimes we take basics for granted. Look back at your "essentials" list. Can you live without any of them? Which ones?

What are you willing to give up for Christ?

"Let us throw off everything that hinders and the sin that so easily entangles, and let us run with perseverance the race marked out for us" (Heb. 12:1). Are you willing to lose a few shackles to fit into His plan for your life?

Paul had few creature comforts, though he may have been in a rented home rather in than a dungeon in Rome (scholars disagree about Paul's Roman prison conditions). He was probably chained to a guard and had to contend with abuse and discomfort daily. Nevertheless, he says, "I am not complaining about having too little. I have learned to be satisfied with whatever I have" (Phil. 4:11). What a statement! I know few people who are totally satisfied. In fact, I know a few people who are not satisfied unless they're miserable. (C'mon, admit it. Don't you know a few like that?)

Switching Roles

Paul begins in verse 12 a series of contrasts. Name them below:

"I know what it is to be poor or to have plenty, and I have lived under all kinds of conditions. I know what it means to be full or to be hungry, to have too much or too little" (Phil. 4:12 CEV).

Friend to Friend

List five essentials (needs) for you now.

1.

2.

3.

4.

5.

List five wants not essential for you now.

1.

2.

3.

4.

5.

Friend to Friend

Which of these contrasting conditions describes you?

CONTRASTS:

_____ / _____

_____ / _____

_____ / _____

When Paul was a wealthy, erudite, high-ranking Jew, he persecuted Christians. He seemed heartless. He showed his religious zeal by killing people. Do you think he had too much? ☐ Yes ☐ No

What do you think "too much" means?

What were Paul's possible motives for his actions when he was a high-ranking religious leader?

How did Paul change over the years?

What did his own persecution teach him?

What should motivate Christian leaders today?

Only for You, Jesus

Barbara Joiner tells the story of a mission trip she took with teenagers. They went to a migrant camp and found a sick mother in bed with a feverish infant. Several small children played in the room, which had not been cleaned in days. Barbara asked the teenagers to begin helping: some to tell a Bible story to the older children, some to change diapers, some to sweep. She asked one teenager to wash the dishes, piled high in the sink and surrounded by dirty, greasy water. This young girl had lived in a spotless house and had never seen such a sink. Barbara rocked the baby and watched the girl grimace as she stuck her clean hand into the dirty water to pull the plug. The girl said, "Only for You, Jesus. Only for You."

Can you say you have been willing to lead others regardless of circumstances, only for Him? Is your motivation always "for Him?" Like Paul, have you been content even in poverty, even in hunger, if it is a sacrifice for Him? Have you been content with Jesus, even when you had too little?

What Do I Know How to Do?

Part of being a godly woman is relinquishing your power to Christ. Consider these two areas of power that you can give to Him: knowledge and experience.

1. KNOWLEDGE IS POWER

Consider what you have to give away for the cause of Christ. What knowledge could you share about Scripture, family life, or other areas?

Lord, I offer You these areas of my knowledge:

2. EXPERIENCE IS POWER

Now consider your experiences that you can give away for the cause of Christ. "Consider it pure joy, my brothers, whenever you face trials of many kinds" (James 1:2). What experiences—good or bad—could you share with others to help them move to spiritual maturity?

Lord, I offer You the following experiences. Please use them to help others.

Right now I have too little
_____ .

Right now I have too much
_____ .

The Mystery of Transformation: Contentment Comes When We Give It Away

Like happiness, contentment is as elusive as a butterfly. You can chase it forever but never catch it. However, when you least expect it, when you forget about capturing it, when you are content to give it away, when you are busy giving away your power to others for the cause of Christ, then contentment lights on your shoulder.

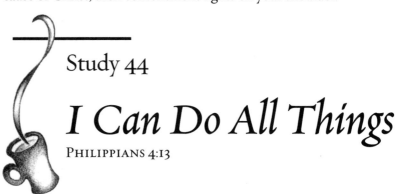

Study 44

I Can Do All Things

PHILIPPIANS 4:13

AT LAST WE HAVE COME TO THE STUDY CONTAINING MY favorite verse! I have been waiting through 43 studies to get to this page in the Bible study. Paul says, "I can do everything through him who gives me strength" (Phil. 4:13). I memorized the verse in this way as a child: "I can do all things through Christ which strengtheneth me" (KJV). Have you ever had a word from God that made you grin all over? This verse does that for me. If I think of it as I drive, I smile, though other drivers may cut me off, stop too short, or slow to make me miss the green light. Speaking as a person of little strength, I am excited about a mighty God who shares His strength with me!

Have you memorized this verse? Write it the way you memorized it.

"Everything" Is a Bit Much!

Whether you translate this verse "everything" or "all things," the concept is a bit much. Can you believe Paul when he says he can do everything through Christ? Whoa, Paul, you're getting a little carried away, there, aren't you?

But look back at the verse. What two key words make this concept possible? _____ _____.

What do you think it means to do everything through Christ?

If you can believe that you, like Paul, can do everything through Christ, then what can limit you?

If God leads you as a leader, then you can lead anything! Only your small vision will limit what you can do.

My Future Is Limited Only by My Watch and Calendar

A few years ago, my job required that all supervisors go on a women's retreat, where the leader asked us to bring our calendars. In the opening session, she asked us to go outside, sit under a tree, pray, and then offer our calendars to God. She asked that we strike any assignment or appointment He told us to delete. I couldn't wait! I knew my calendar was too full. I never had understood some of those "opportunities for service," and I couldn't wait to strike them. To my surprise, I did not get rid of anything. As I held up my calendar, offering it to God, He warmed my heart to each assignment. He even added one thing I needed to do that year.

Offer your calendar to God today. Ask Him to show you what to add and what to delete. Offer Him your time. Ask Him to bless each minute, hour, and day. Ask Him to guard the time and give you the priorities you need in planning.

If I Can Do All Things, Which Will I Choose?

Now here's the good part of calendar planning for an almighty God who said you can do everything through Him: you get to choose! He gives you free will, and you can prioritize your life. You can choose to watch TV, read a novel, or commit adultery with your neighbor's spouse. Or you can pray, read your Bible, and give your food to hungry people at a community soup kitchen. What's your vision?

Open the Treasure Chest

Let's review Colossians 2:2–3: "My purpose is that they may be encouraged in heart and united in love, so that they may have the full riches of complete understanding, in order that they may know

Try this exercise with your calendar as described in the paragraph to the left.

Friend to Friend

Fill in your friend's name and read this paragraph to her for her encouragement.

the mystery of God, namely, Christ, in whom are hidden all the treasures of wisdom and knowledge." What a wonderful purpose Paul has. He wants you to be encouraged in heart and united with other Christians in love. His wants you to have full spiritual riches! "I will give you the treasures of darkness, riches stored in secret places, so that you may know that I am the LORD, the God of Israel, who summons you by name" (Isaiah 45:3).

Write your name in the blanks below. Then read aloud

I, the Lord, summon you, _____, by name. I

want you to have all My spiritual wealth, dear _____.

Be encouraged. Unite with other Christians to serve Me, and I will

give you, _____ the treasure stored in secret places,

so that you may know that I am your Lord.

Notice the three words in Colossians 2 that pertain to head knowledge/thinking/planning:

1. Knowledge: God wants you to use your mind to uncover facts.
2. Understanding: He wants you to comprehend, knowing why.
3. Wisdom: He wants you to have the capacity to choose well.

When Paul was in Philippi, he decided to go to Jerusalem. The Philippians asked him not to go. They based their decision on the facts: Paul had enemies in Jerusalem. Paul prayed. He gained understanding: God said go, so he went. He went, was arrested, and the missionary work of the greatest missionary in his day came to an end. In the end, he dies. Yet, God worked through him in Rome, a strategic city. Over the next years, the Roman Empire spread Christianity all over the world. If you are a Christian, you are an inheritor of that strong church in Rome that survived, kept Scriptures alive, and still exists today. If the Philippians had foreseen the wisdom in Paul's decision, they would have said, "Go on, Paul." Then they may have looked up and whispered, "Only for You, Jesus. Only for You."

Things in the Attic

When Paul speaks of "everything" in Philippians 4:13, did he think of my "to do" list? Maybe as you've studied this verse, you've also thought you can't do everything through Him until you throw out a few things already on your list. Do you have things hidden in your attic that need to be thrown away? Toss them. Then drag out all those things you've thought of doing for Christ but you never had time to do. Bring them to the forefront. Ask God for the knowledge, understanding, and wisdom to plan well.

The Mystery of Transformation: Jesus Is a Treasure Chest of "All Things"

Spend time now praising God for His Son, Jesus, the treasure chest of hidden knowledge, understanding, and wisdom. Though you don't understand the mystery, ask Him for discernment as He transforms your calendar and your time, enabling you to set priorities and do all things—the things you thought you'd never be able to do!

Study 45

Communication Skills

PHILIPPIANS 4:14–15

I HAD JUST MOVED TO A SMALL, ONE-BEDROOM APARTMENT IN a large city in a neighborhood I didn't know. Come to think of it, I didn't know anyone in the entire state. I went to church my first Sunday in town and met Sue, a friendly young woman. She came over several times; I went to her home and met her parents. I shared that I was a widow and had left my college-aged children in my home state to take a ministry position in the new city.

Times were hard those first few years. I had taken a one-third cut in pay compared with my schoolteaching salary, yet I had decided to follow Jesus—without any other friend—to this place I

Friend to Friend

How would you respond if someone shared with you the way Sue did?

felt sure He was leading me. One day near Christmas I answered the door. Sue stood there, pointing to an envelope taped to the door. We opened it and found fifty dollars inside. "Where'd this come from?" she asked.

"I have no idea," I replied.

Four years later my daughter married. Expenses were more than I expected. After praying about it, I went to Sue and asked for a loan. She gave it to me immediately, and when I asked about a schedule for repayment, she reminded me of these words: "And if you lend to those from whom you expect repayment, what credit is that to you? . . . Lend to them without expecting to get anything back" (Luke 6:34–35). She said, "I trust that God sent you to me. I gave you all I have in my checking account. I believe this is the right thing to do. Do not pay me back." She paused and smiled. "Well, if God blesses you and you have it to spare one day, then give it to me, but don't make partial payments or feel guilty because you owe it. That will destroy our friendship in Christ. I am not expecting it back. I mean that. I believe God's word, which says, 'Good will come to him who is generous and lends freely, who conducts his affairs with justice'" (Ps. 112:5).

Years later, after I had moved from that city to California and then back to the South, God allowed my path to cross Sue's again. She generously let me housesit in her beautiful home for several years while she was on assignment across the country. She made it possible for me to do the ministry God had called me to do—and she did it in a spirit of generosity.

What a joy to have a friend like Sue! God has blessed me in many ways by allowing our friendship, not to mention that of her dear mother, Juanita, now also a widow.

Paul had just finished saying he can live independently, making a little money on the side as he goes, learning to be content when he "abounds" or suffers with little. He can do all things through Christ. I imagine he paused after writing that and thought, "Now, wait a minute. I'm not too independent! I need other people and don't want to lose my good friends!" He then writes to the Philippians, who sent him food and money, "Yet it was good of you to share in my troubles" (Phil. 4:14).

The King James Version of Philippians 4:14 translates "share in my troubles" (above) as "communicate with my affliction." What a way to communicate! Most people in need cannot hear the gospel message on an empty stomach. Until you take care of their basic needs, you cannot communicate to them who Jesus is. Once they see you care by filling their stomachs, then their eyes and ears are open to observe your Christian witness.

Let's review what we learned earlier in this Philippians study: Paul took his first missionary trip through Philippi (a city in Macedonia—now modern Turkey), establishing a church there. When he later departed to continue spreading the gospel, he left many friends in Philippi who cared deeply about him. When they heard he was imprisoned in Rome, they were one of the few groups who ministered to his needs by sending not only food, money, and perhaps some clothing but also Epaphroditus, a companion who could minister to Paul. Until he later became sick and had to return to Philippi, Epaphroditus became Paul's servant. He brought items of comfort to fill Paul's needs.

In this Scripture, Paul remembers leaving Philippi for the first time: "Moreover, as you Philippians know, in the early days of your acquaintance with the gospel [on Paul's first missionary journey], when I set out from Macedonia [actually, from the area of Philippi], not one church shared with me ["communicated with" me (KJV)] in the matter of giving and receiving, except you only" (Phil. 4:15).

How did the Philippians minister to Paul's needs? They sent

1.

2.

3.

4.

Did you list food, money, clothing, a servant/friend, kind words, a note, or other things? You may remember when someone contributed to your needs. How?

Friend to Friend

Have you ever had a friend who generously shared in your troubles?
☐ Yes ☐ No

How did she/he share in your joy as well as in your troubles?

In verse 15 Paul speaks of "the matter of _____ and _____." What do you think the Philippians received from Paul?

Paul communicated the greatest gift, the message of the gospel: that Jesus Christ died as a sacrifice for their sins and that as He was resurrected to live forever, so could they, with Him in their hearts. What a wonderful gift he gave: living words!

Words Spoken Cannot Be Retracted

You may feel sad or inadequate because you have no extravagant gifts for others. However, like Paul, you can give encouraging, uplifting words. What kind of words have you communicated lately—or today?

Gift two people with encouraging words today. Tell your study partner what it was like.

Do you wish you had kept your mouth closed today? You have within you the power to give positive words that make a difference in the lives of others. Paul gave words of blessing and encouragement, even when he had no money to give. In another incident with a lame man, Peter summarized Paul's attitude: "'Silver or gold I do not have, but what I have I give you'" (Acts 3:6). Decide now what kind of words or other gifts you can share to encourage others.

"Well Done" Affirmation

Look back at verse 15. Paul says, "Not one church shared with me in the matter of giving and receiving, except you only." These are encouraging words of affirmation from Paul.

From other words in this verse, how do you learn that when the Philippians shared so generously, they were not mature Christians?

You do not have to be a perfect, mature Christian to affirm others through your God-given gifts. At any stage of maturity, use what He has given you.

The Mystery of Transformation: Jesus' Communication Is Miraculous

Try this exercise now: communicate your joy to a friend without speaking a word. You can do it through silent body language. Jesus communicates with us sometimes in the silence. Take a few moments now to listen to Him in the silence. Later, practice daily silent listening, and then thank Him for His miraculous communication through His "still small voice" (1 Kings 19:12 KJV) as He transforms your heart in the quiet.

Unit 10:

Lord, I'm Fruitful and Fragrant. Am I Ready?

■ ■ ■ ■ WHEN GOD SAYS YOU CAN DO ALL THINGS through Christ, He means it! You have arrived at the finish line. You have five baby steps to go before you finish this Bible study. As you close this Bible study, respond to God by

> exercising your spiritual fruits and gifts,
> offering Him the sweet aroma of your sacrifice,
> trusting Him to supply all your needs,
> living a life of civility for the Prince of Peace,
> and trusting in His amazing grace.

God's Word always calls searchers to a higher place, a higher plane of living. If this Bible study has not enriched your life and caused a change in you, then it has failed. O godly woman, please allow your Savior to be absolute Lord of your life. Live as a "living letter, written on our hearts, known and read by everybody." May God bless you in special ways as you cross the finish line. Now turn the page and go for it!

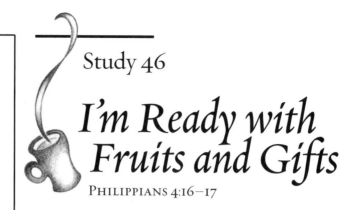

Study 46

I'm Ready with Fruits and Gifts

PHILIPPIANS 4:16–17

AT FOURTEEN I WAS IMPRESSED BY BIG GIFTS—THE BIGGER, the better. On Valentine's Day, my boyfriend always gave me flowers or a box of candy. Two roses were better than one. If I got a dozen roses, then the guy was fantastic! The man I married gave me orchids and large boxes of chocolates with nuts and fruit fillings. What a man!

Now I'm older and wiser. I know gifts are not the measure of a person's character. I understand that large boxes of chocolates do not a relationship make.

Paul may have agreed with the English poet Richard Lovelace that "Stone walls do not a prison make, Nor iron bars a cage." While in prison, his spirit soared free, filled at times with remarkable joy. He appreciated gifts the Philippians sent: "For even when I was in Thessalonica, you sent me aid again and again when I was in need" (Phil. 4:16). Paul probably knew this Proverb well: "A gift opens the way for the giver and ushers him into the presence of the great" (Proverbs 18:16). Can you picture a traveler at a king's palace, pulling out lavish gifts, giving them to the gatekeeper, and then being ushered into the presence of the king?

Paul quickly corrects any idea that he had to beg or that his King needed the Philippians' gifts to spread the gospel. God was powerful enough to do that. "Not that I am looking for a gift, but I am looking for what may be credited to your account" (Phil. 4:17). Paul didn't keep tally on what the Philippians gave, but he recognized their sacrifice and knew God honored it as worthy. "I want you to receive the blessings that come from giving" (Phil. 4:17). You may enjoy giving to others for the blessings you receive.

Unique Spiritual Gifts

God gives us spiritual and physical gifts. Paul identifies some spiritual gifts Christians use to build the body of Christ, His church: "There are different kinds of gifts, but the same Spirit" (1 Cor. 12:4). Paul then lists these gifts: the message of wisdom, the message of knowledge, faith, healing, miraculous powers, prophecy, distinguishing between spirits, speaking in different kinds of tongues, and interpretation of tongues (1 Cor. 12:8–10).

Later Paul says, "Now you are the body of Christ, and each one of you is a part of it. And in the church God has appointed first of all apostles, second prophets, third teachers, then workers of miracles, also those having gifts of healing, those able to help others, those with gifts of administration, and those speaking in different kinds of tongues" (1 Cor. 12:27–28). Paul also writes: "We have different gifts, according to the grace given us. If a man's gift is prophesying, let him use it in proportion to his faith. If it is serving, let him serve; if it is teaching, let him teach; if it is encouraging, let him encourage; if it is contributing to the needs of others, let him give generously; if it is leadership, let him govern diligently; if it is showing mercy, let him do it cheerfully" (Rom. 12:6–8).

Choosing and Using Your Gifts

As you use your gifts, others in your church will recognize them. If you have the gift of hospitality, people will enjoy and appreciate church socials in your home. If you have the gift of administration, the nominating committee may find you a place on the finance committee.

What is most important about your church?

Are you satisfied with the way it is handled? ☐ Yes ☐ No

If you used your spiritual gifts, what could you do?

Look at the verses to the left, circling a few gifts He has given you. It may be hard to recognize your gifts.

Ask your study partner or a friend to help you identify them here:

Friend to Friend

My vow to God: Lord, I will give You the gift of_____
_____, which You gave me to serve Your church.

It would take more pages than this book contains to explain all the gifts. For deeper study, read *Yours for the Giving*, by Barbara Joiner (available from New Hope Publishers), and use the gifts inventory to identify your gifts. You may want to work through "Me Gifted?" from *Woman to Woman: Preparing Yourself to Mentor*, pp. 7–12 (also available from New Hope Publishers).

Fruits of the Spirit

As we obey Him by using our gifts, our spirits will grow fruit. Paul said to Timothy, whom he was mentoring, "The husbandman [gardener] that laboreth must be first partaker of the fruits" (2 Tim. 2:6 KJV). Jesus said, "'Every tree that does not produce good fruit will be cut down and thrown into the fire'" (Luke 3:9). "'No good tree bears bad fruit, nor does a bad tree bear good fruit. Each tree is recognized by its own fruit. People do not pick figs from thornbushes, or grapes from briers. The good man brings good things out of the good stored up in his heart, and the evil man brings evil things out of the evil stored up in his heart. For out of the overflow of his heart his mouth speaks'" (Luke 6:43–45).

I used to think the fruit I should produce was a group of other Christians whom I had led to know Jesus. However, God has shown me that my witnessing or good deeds have nothing to do with bearing fruit. His Holy Spirit within me grows the fruit: "But the fruit of the Spirit is love, joy, peace, patience, kindness, goodness, faithfulness, gentleness and self-control" (Gal. 5:22–23). As I yield to Him who dwells inside me, these things become a part of my personality—my whole self. I overflow with love, joy, peace, and all the rest of the fruit of the Spirit, as He grows them in my heart.

Jesus said, "'By their fruit you will recognize them'" (Matt. 7:16).

• Don't feel proud, godly woman, if you can name a thousand people whom you've led to know Jesus as Savior. You can't count them as evidence that you are worthy of heaven. You didn't do the work; the Spirit did.

Circle the fruits that you show. Ask a friend to add or subtract.

love

joy

peace

patience

kindness

goodness

faithfulness

gentleness

self-control

What do you think happens to self-righteous people?

• Don't feel guilty, fellow Christian, fearing God will cut you down because you can't name those thousand people. This is not the fruit He speaks of. It's sad when people brag about how much they give, how many people they've "won," and what rewards they'll have in heaven—when we see only a mean spirit and unmerciful haughtiness inside them. They do not have the fruit of the Spirit, as far as anyone can tell.

"Produce, then, fruit that is consistent with the repentance you profess" (Matt. 3:8 Williams). Since you accepted Jesus, His Spirit has been growing fruit in you. Let it grow.

Used to Serve Christ

"Let us hold unswervingly to the hope we profess, for he who promised is faithful. And let us consider how we may spur one another on toward love and good deeds" (Heb. 10:23–24). I'll never forget the day in a California women's camp cabin when Marie asked to receive Jesus. Our leader, Jean, burst through the door, did an immediate turnaround, and went to the porch to pray for us. She knew her job in the body of Christ. Jean's prayers of intercession were important to that sacred moment, as the Spirit spoke to Marie.

     Yes, every Christian should witness, but all of us, using our gifts together, will accomplish that purpose. That's the way the Body works!

The Mystery of Transformation: You Are a Special Delight

Here's the mystery of this study: Our gifts to God do not usher us into heaven. His gifts to us are more important, as we use them in the body of Christ. He gives us His fruit: love, joy, peace, patience, kindness, goodness, faithfulness, gentleness, and self-control. As they overflow from our faithful hearts, we are transformed into special delights, like chocolate candy with fruit filling inside.

Unit Ten • 181

Study 47

I'm Ready with Aromas and Fragrances

PHILIPPIANS 4:18

NOTHING SMELLS BETTER THAN THE AROMAS COMING FROM a church kitchen where good cooks are preparing a celebrative dinner. Years ago, I belonged to a church renowned for its chef. With just the right spices, she carefully prepared meals with a flair for presentation. She displayed special foods customized for adults, youth, and children. One Wednesday afternoon, a church staff member smelled a pungent aroma coming from the kitchen and decided to sneak a taste. He sipped the deep-green soup from the large pot on the stove. About that time a volunteer came down the hall, shouting, "Hey, what do you think of that for the children's play?"

"It's tasty, but it needs salt," he replied.

"Ugh!" she said. "That is the green dye for our forest backdrop."

Food is important in today's church. Did you read this email joke last Christmas? If the three wise men had been women, then instead of gold, frankincense, and myrrh, they would have brought diapers, a broom, and a tasty casserole! In most churches, we can hardly survive without casseroles. In your church the candles at Christmas, lilies at Easter, and other smells around the sanctuary may also fill you with fragrant memories.

Paul also has fragrant memories as he remembers the gifts of the Philippians. They were a poor group, and he knew each gift represented sacrifice from their small resources. "I have received full payment and even more; I am amply supplied, now that I have received from Epaphroditus the gifts you sent. They are a fragrant offering, an acceptable sacrifice, pleasing to God" (Phil. 4:18). Paul is sitting in chains, yet he has cause to rejoice: he has plenty because they were generous. All he gave the Philippians seems little compared to their sacrifice.

List a few aromas that trigger happy memories for you.

Worshipping and Smelling

Church kitchen smells are usually a long way from the sanctuary, but in Paul's day worship included the strong odor of incense in the temple. Worshippers smelled the wonderful aroma of meat and wine cooking on the altar, almost like a barbecue—not to mention the smells of animal stalls and dove cages in the outer courtyard. Also, these days came before toothbrushes or deodorant, so you can imagine the smells emanating from the worshippers!

Temples in the land of Palestine were probably not comfortable places most of the time, with a hot fire before the congregation for the sacrifices of bread, meat, and wine. Only priests from the Levite tribe could eat these sacrifices dedicated to God. However, ordinary worshippers in the early church participated in many fellowship meals. Besides using the bread and wine of communion (as we use today), they enjoyed several religious festivals with food, such as the seven-day Feast of Unleavened Bread, the Feast of Harvest for the first crops that came in, and the Feast of Ingathering at the end of the harvest season (Ex. 23:14–17).

Bethany was the scene of many dinners with Jesus and his friends Mary, Martha, and Lazarus. As they fellowshipped with each other, they communed with God. I can imagine that Jesus was the life of the party, the living Lord, offering living water on many occasions. His first miracle was at a wedding party, where He turned the water into wine (John 2:1–11). Jesus was concerned about human need. He often broke bread and blessed it for His friends, and He fed thousands on a grassy hillside with a few fish and barley loaves. Then, near the end of His life on earth, He celebrated a meal called the Last Supper in an upper room with His disciples.

God Provides the Greatest Sacrifice

Look back at Paul's words in Philippians 4:18: "I have received full

_____ and even more; I am amply _____, now

that I have _____ from Epaphroditus the

_____ you sent. They are a fragrant _____, an

acceptable sacrifice, pleasing to God."

What fragrances make you think of your church?

The words you filled in are important in describing the process of sacrifice: payment/supplied/received/gifts/offering. Let's explore them further.

God set the scene for sacrifice when He asked Abraham to offer his son, Isaac, as a burnt offering. Years before, God had promised Abraham abundant descendants, but even in his old age, he had none. Then his wife, Sara, (who was 90) conceived and gave birth to a precious child. Imagine God asking for such a sacrifice, especially from someone who had waited so long for the promise to come true! Genesis 22 records the story: After God asked for Isaac as a sacrifice, Abraham wasted no time. He rose early in the morning (Gen. 22:3) and went to the place where God showed him. He even laid the wood for a fire, tied Isaac down, and got out his knife to kill him (Gen. 22:10). Then God spoke: "'Do not lay a hand on the boy,' he said. 'Do not do anything to him. Now I know that you fear God, because you have not withheld from me your son, your only son.'" God provided a ram that day as the sacrifice, and then He gave Abraham an affirmation that his descendants would become a great nation, Israel.

Jewish people told this story for centuries as an example of God's love and their obedience. Later God fulfilled the story, sending Jesus, His only Son, whom He loved, to die for us. He was willing to offer the sacrifice because He loved us, just as Abraham was willing to offer his sacrifice because he loved and trusted God. God still gives us promises. He loves you enough to offer His most precious Son as a *payment* for your sins, to *supply* the redemption for you (like green stamps you redeem, or claim), so you can go to heaven. You *receive* the blessing of heaven as a free *gift*, an *offering* of love you don't have to earn or pay for!

Acceptable and Pleasing to God

As you near the finish line in the race to complete this Bible study, think of the impact of the principles God has taught you. You may be tired and ready to hit the ribbon at the end of the race. You may be sweaty and a little smelly like those worshippers around the fire in the Palestine temple. It has not been easy, but take heart. You have only three more studies before this Bible study concludes. You're going to be a winner, because God has sacrificed to give you the greatest prize of all.

Explain the concept of sacrifice in your own words.

The Mystery of Transformation:
From Raw Ingredients to a Finished Presentation

Paul says our sacrifice is a fragrant aroma to God. As you run the race toward heaven, you will sacrifice. Someone may throw a few "rotten tomatoes" at you along the way. You may strain a muscle and perhaps stop for a rest. Yet, as you obey, God mysteriously changes you. As your church cook changes a recipe, He transforms your raw ingredients—who you are today—into a finished presentation fit for the King.

Study 48

Supplying Out of a Rich Storehouse

PHILIPPIANS 4:19

I WORK IN A BUILDING THAT HAS A GIANT WAREHOUSE ON ONE side. Inside the warehouse are huge shelves that stretch to the ceiling. Warehouse workers drive large forklift trucks that pick up large wooden flats of products and take them to the shipping dock. It's a large operation. They also have a machine that shrink-wraps large bundles of magazines before shipping them to customers. The amount of merchandise in the warehouse is overwhelming. Yet, our warehouse handles only the backorders and special mailings. The main shipments of our magazines, books, and other products go straight from the printer to customers. What a huge operation! However, I know an even larger operation: God's universe. To supply it, He keeps a rich storehouse. Think on this: He owns everything— everything in my company's warehouse, everything in the larger printer's warehouse, everything in every warehouse in the world, and even more. If you started counting everything God owns, you'd never finish the list. He owns all the riches in the universe.

Paul knew full well God's supply house. He had seen it in

action. He says, "And my God will meet all your needs according to his glorious riches in Christ Jesus" (Phil. 4:19).

Begin with My God

Read this verse again, and write the word just before "God."

Whose God owns all the glorious riches in the world?

Have you ever watched several grandchildren climb into their grandmother's lap? My friend Debra Berry has a childhood memory of climbing into her grandmother's lap. Usually one of the grandchildren patted her and said, "My grandmother." Another child then said, "No, *my* grandmother," and another would shout, *"No! My grandmother!"* Our situation with God is similar: He is your Heavenly Father, but He's also mine. In addition, He is the Heavenly Father of her, and her, and him, and her, and them, and . . . every child of God.

Read the verse again, and fill in these blanks:

"And _____ God _____ meet all _____ according to his _____ riches in _____ _____" (Phil. 4:19).

After you've finished filling in the first two blanks, explain what you think these words mean: My God will

Whose needs will He meet?

Yes, He will meet your needs. What about someone who sits on a crowded street and begs in Bangladesh? Will He meet her needs?

How does this verse say He will meet your needs?

What kinds of riches does God have?

Today we don't think as much as we used to about all God's riches. It may be that we are too rich with material things to dwell on God's riches—our riches keep us too busy. Even if you consider yourself poor, you may not be as poor as your grandmother or a beggar in Bangladesh.

Heaven and the Streets of Gold

When I was a little girl, I memorized this verse, "But my God shall supply all your need according to his riches in glory by Christ Jesus" (Phil. 4:19 KJV). I thought of "glory" as a place—heaven. My mother's generation spoke often of the pearly gates and the streets of gold in heaven. They talked about the crystal sea beside the golden city, the New Jerusalem. Even in my generation we sang about "mansions in glory" and that "I've got a home in glory land that outshines the sun!"

List some other ideas about "glory" that songs describe.

What Are the Riches in God's Warehouse?

Donald Trump, Bill Gates, Ross Perot, all the Rockefellers, the Vanderbilts, and the Fortune 500 stockholders put together have only pennies compared to the wealth in God's warehouse. What an awesome God; His riches are glorious!

Take a final look at Phil. 4:19: "And my God will meet all your needs according to his glorious riches in Christ Jesus."

Jesus, the Provider, Gatekeeper to the Storehouse

Here is the key to understanding this verse: "in Christ Jesus."

God is not speaking of His physical wealth, although He owns all of it—gold, silver, diamonds, iron ore, everything in the ground, everything on it, and everything high above it. He is speaking of His spiritual wealth. The supernatural Jesus can meet every

Friend to Friend

If you had all the money in the world, what would you do with it? Name your top ten priorities.

spiritual need you have, including the ultimate need for salvation. He does not promise to supply all our physical needs. If He did, you could expect perfect eyesight, smooth-working joints, and a brain that never forgets. You could expect that no disease would ever attack a family member and that none would develop signs of old age. You could expect that He would eliminate all beggars in Bangladesh and all over the world.

You could expect more money to pay your bills, to give to family, and to give to deserving charitable organizations. However, God does not promise to give our greedy hearts all we would try to grasp. He promises that, in His perfect will, He will meet our ultimate need, the need for salvation and hope.

God promises an inheritance more precious than any of the world's wealth: "An inheritance that can never perish, spoil or fade—kept in heaven for you, who through faith are shielded by God's power until the coming of the salvation that is ready to be revealed in the last time. In this you greatly rejoice, though now for a little while you may have had to suffer grief in all kinds of trials. These have come so that your faith—of greater worth than gold, which perishes even though refined by fire—may be proved genuine and may result in praise, glory and honor when Jesus Christ is revealed" (1 Peter 1:4–7).

Spend time praising and honoring Him by singing "More Precious Than Silver" and "I'd Rather Have Jesus," if you know these choruses.

The Mystery of Transformation: Jesus Transforms My Needs into Gold

In 1 Chronicles 28, David tells his son Solomon how to build the Jerusalem temple. He sets priorities of gold and silver for all the items of worship in the temple. Some wooden items he places in the back. Some he covers with silver and places in the middle. The most precious items, covered with the purest gold, he places right in the front of the worship room. You are a priority to God. He cares about you and mysteriously transforms you from a lackluster, needy beggar into a Christian with a heart of pure gold.

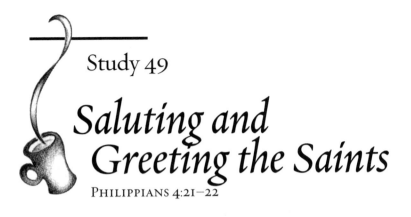

Study 49

Saluting and Greeting the Saints

PHILIPPIANS 4:21–22

SEVERAL WEEKS AGO, MY PASTOR TOLD THE FOLLOWING STORY: He was traveling to a conference and checked into a hotel. A man in line at the hotel desk gave his name to the clerk, who responded, "I'm sorry, sir, but we do not have your reservation." The man became angry and lashed out at the clerk, who said, "No problem, sir. We have plenty of rooms. I'll register you now." The man's wife was embarrassed and tried to calm him, but he did not hear her. Apparently, he did not hear the clerk, either, for he complained loudly about not having his reservations honored and not having a room when he arrived. He was so busy firing off expletives that he could not hear anyone. Shouting, he asked to speak to the manager, while his wife still tried to calm him. When the manager finally settled the matter, offering him the keys to the room he had all along, the man stormed off, tripped over his suitcase, and fell. Those watching could hardly control their laughter. The man had lost his cool. Consequently, he looked ridiculous.

Christians can learn a good principle here: anger makes you deaf and blind. When you are angry and absorbed in a negative mindset, you cannot hear what others say, so you appear foolish. You might say the daggers in your eyes (or the hot blood) make you blind.

Be positive! Be civil!

After his magnificent statement of faith in God's provision for all his needs (Study 48), Paul begins to close this letter to the Philippians in the usual polite way, much like we end a letter or email today: "Everybody here says hello. Give my love to all." Paul says, "Greet all the saints in Christ Jesus. The brothers who are with me send greetings. All the saints send you greetings, especially those who belong to Caesar's household" (Phil. 4:21–22). Paul, who had a reason to lash out at the world, remains calm to the end. As a true leader, he sets an example of positive, optimistic faith and civility before the Philippian church.

"Greet all the saints" can be translated "Salute every saint" (KJV). Paul affirms the Philippians and shows them respect as he closes his love letter to them. He has poured out his heart to his friends, and, like a retiring general, salutes his troops—those who will carry on the mission after he is gone. As you probably know, "the saints" describes all Christians—those who have a relationship with the living Lord. To be a saint, you do not have to be a perfect, moral person who never makes mistakes. You are a saint if you accept Jesus into your heart to cleanse you and make you like Him. Don't be modest; step up to sainthood!

Begin with Saintly Children

Because I am a saint, I will do these things for my family members: (List the names, and write your commitment beside each name.)

As a saint, you begin to grow more like Him. You mature, baby step by baby step, making progress as the Holy Spirit indwells you. You become more saintly because your Savior within you is sinless and pure. Jesus says, "'You will know that I am in union with my Father and you are in union with me and I am in union with you'" (John 14:20 Williams). Out of a faithful heart you want to serve Him, to begin living a controlled life of civility. Your positive, ethical, spirit of civility and self-control flows from you to your family. You set an example before your children. Instead of screaming and hitting, they can say "please" and "thank you" at an early age, because their mother lives on a higher plane than a non-Christian mother does. Your husband, parents, and friends will begin to see the difference, as you become a clearer reflection of the Prince of Peace.

Remember, you are a saint, not because you have earned sainthood but because Jesus' Spirit lives within you. His Spirit is always contagious. You may not see it immediately, but your family will discern it as it proves itself lasting. The Light of the world is bright. You cannot hide it for long. It will shine from your personality as surely as the sun comes up each morning. Only your willful disobedience will prevent that light from shining in you—if you refuse to allow Christ's light to permeate your entire heart. I beg you; don't say no to Him because of false humility or false pride. Go ahead; accept that you are a saint because of Him, and then act like it!

A Call to a Higher Place

Are you ready to accept a higher calling, to step up and get a better perspective on life?

The psalmist says, "Lead me to the rock that is higher than I" (Ps. 61:2). In the northernmost point in Europe, in the small town of Albec, Denmark, an old lighthouse steered ships home for years. However, over time, the sand shifted, and the old lighthouse was no longer high enough for ships to see. Mounds of shifting sand hid it. Sometimes you need to clear away the sand and dirt before you can reflect the light. God calls you to be a beacon to others, to stand tall as His saint, with the light inside shining brightly.

Here's the dirt I need to clear away:

Because Paul had cleared away the dirt in his life, he reflected only the clear light of Jesus. Notice in Philippians 4:22 whose household he mentions:

"All the _____ send you greetings, especially those who

belong to _____ 's household.

Paul could influence the palace of Caesar, the most powerful person in the known world at that time. There is no telling what influence you can have, when you step up to sainthood.

The Mystery of Transformation: God Shines from Inside Me

Think about this mystery: you are sinful and imperfect, yet you are a saint. You are yourself—unique and special—yet God Himself has sent His Spirit to live within you, if you're a Christian. He respects you and never violates your will, yet He wants you to have the courage to live as a saint. He will not ask you to do anything without His Spirit leading you, yet He will move you up and out to live on a higher plane, closer to Him. As He transforms you, He allows you to reflect the Light of the world.

Share with your study partner about the dirt you need to clear away.

Study 50

Grace with You

PHILIPPIANS 4:23

GOOD-BYES ARE NEVER EASY. IF YOU HAVE BEEN WORKING through this Bible study for weeks with a dear friend, you are coming to the end of the last unit together. You may decide to study another book of the Bible right away, or you may say "good-bye" after your last session and never spend much time together again. Each of you may teach another friend what you have learned through this book, multiplying your knowledge of Philippians. Either way, you cannot duplicate the closeness you have experienced during this study.

When our oldest child, Jack, left for college, his father and I sat down with him and said, "Remember who you are and whose you are. You can find anything you look for in college. We hope you will look for the right things." We gave him about twenty minutes of good advice, and after he left, we looked at each other sadly, thinking we might never see him again. We had heard other parents tell tearful stories of how their children planned holidays with others, and they hardly came home once they went to college. We should not have worried. Jack left that Monday and returned Thursday, with all his dirty laundry.

Tearful Goodbyes

Paul reluctantly says good-bye in his letter to the Philippians: "The grace of the Lord Jesus Christ be with your spirit. Amen" (Phil. 4:23). He was well aware he might never see them again, since he was imprisoned and facing death in Rome. The Bible is full of similar farewell letters and scenes. Remember the poignant scene in Ruth, where the widowed Naomi says good-bye to her two daughters-in-law, Ruth and Orpah, whose husbands also had died.

What is your "goodbye" style? Share with your study partner some stories of significant goodbyes in your life.

Preparing to return to her hometown, Bethlehem, she unselfishly asked the two young women to go back to their parents. "'Go back, each of you, to your mother's home. May the LORD show kindness to you.' . . . Then she kissed them and they wept aloud and said to her, 'We will go back with you to your people'" (Ruth 1:8–10). Reluctantly, Orpah left in tears (Ruth 1:14), but Ruth refused to go, saying, "'Where you go I will go, and where you stay I will stay. Your people will be my people and your God my God. Where you die I will die'" (Ruth 1:16–17). Ruth could not bear to say good-bye to Naomi, even facing the unknown and living as a foreigner in Palestine.

Taking up the Mantle

Good-byes don't leave us simply to grieve. We have a job to do. Near a place called Gilgal, old Elijah and young Elisha, whom Elijah had mentored, talked about the end of their relationship. Elijah, who knew he was near the end of his life on earth, told young Elisha to stay at Gilgal alone. Elisha refused, saying several times, "'I will not leave you'" (2 Kings 2:2,4,6). Their parting was traumatic: Elisha cried out, "'My father! My father!'" (2 Kings 2:12), as he watched a chariot and horses of fire separate them and then a whirlwind take Elijah up to heaven. After Elijah was gone, Elisha took up the cloak, or mantle, that had fallen from Elijah. Elisha also took up his mentor's ministry. He performed miracles, just as Elijah had done. Prophets from Jericho, who were watching, said, "The spirit of Elijah is resting on Elisha" (2 Kings 2:15). (For more information on Elijah and Elisha's mentoring relationship, read *Seeking Wisdom: Preparing Yourself to Be Mentored* by Edna Ellison and Tricia Scribner.)

Building Fellowship and Ending It

After a Bible study is over, you may end the fellowship with your Bible study partner, but I hope you will never separate yourself from the principles you learn. Paul never forgot those close to him with whom he had shared the Word of God. They were still joined in their hearts, though they were miles apart. You can take what you have learned from Paul's love letter and share it with others in distant places—or share it outside your own back door.

Spend some time with your study partner, sharing how she has helped you and blessed your life.

Discuss how you want to relate in the future. Bless each other as you end this study.

The Grace That Never Ends

Read again Philippians 4:23. What does Paul wish will remain in the spirit of the Philippians?

You can compare "grace" to the unmerited love parents have for their children. No matter how unkind, unruly, and ungrateful the children are, the parents love them, almost unconditionally. When my husband died, I was in my early forties. As soon as the funeral was over, my mother and father came to my home and began to parent me, something they had not done in twenty years! My father took me to the probate judge to make legal arrangements. He gave me financial advice and social advice. Mother gave me suggestions on rearing my children, organizing the household, and facing grief. I had always been close to them but never quite that close. I realized that parenting never ends. As long as you are alive and your children are alive, you feel that unconditional love and responsibility for them. Years later, when my mother was eighty-six years old, she still loved me and put my welfare above hers. That kind of love and grace is amazing. It remains in the spirit.

"Grace" also denotes power—strength to live the Christian life, to serve and praise Him. Paul ended his second letter to Timothy, saying, "The Lord be with your spirit. Grace be with you" (2 Tim. 4:22) The message, "Grace be with you," is the most powerful way to end a relationship—or a letter between Christians. When you come to the end of a treasured period in life, remember that you are not alone. The power goes with you.

Amazing Grace Addressed Personally

In another letter, Paul wrote the people at Corinth: "You yourselves are our letter, written on our hearts, known and read by everybody. . . . You are a letter from Christ . . . written not with ink but with the Spirit of the living God" (2 Cor. 3:2–3).

Write your commitment before God to become His living letter.

Friend to Friend

Amen and What It Means

When I was a child, I wondered if "Amen" and "Selah" had the same meaning. I had seen them both at the end of verses, especially in the Psalms. I later learned at church that "Selah," for the music director, signaled a pause, crescendo, or a musical interlude. We seldom sang the word "Amen"; it was an ending, usually to a prayer or a blessing, meaning, "Let it be so!" I like to translate "Amen" as "Oh, yeah!" Paul ends his beautiful letter to his beloved Philippians by wishing them the best of the best: the grace of their living Lord in their loving hearts. Oh, yeah!

The Mystery of Transformation: Jesus Has Amazing Grace!

Here's the most amazing mystery of all: God is transforming you, even now. After you finish this study, you can still depend on His promise that He will never leave you or forsake you (Heb. 13:5). You can "be transformed by the renewing of your mind" (Rom. 12:2). You never get too old to learn and to know God better. The almighty, living God continually reaches down from heaven to lift up you and me and change us, and we soar with Him in the power of His grace as His joyful, godly servants! Oh, yeah!

Talk with your study partner about how you have experienced transformation during this study.

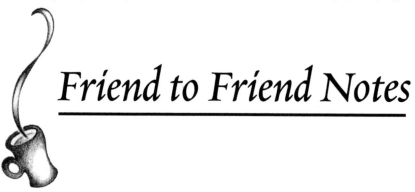

Friend to Friend Notes

Friend to Friend Notes

Friend to Friend Notes

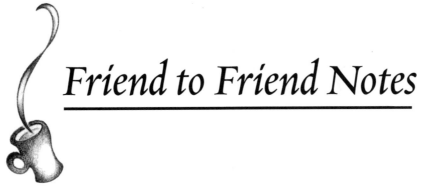

Friend to Friend Notes

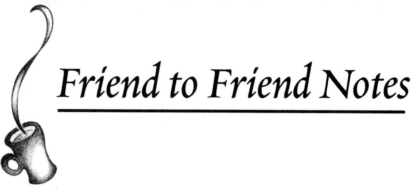

Friend to Friend Notes

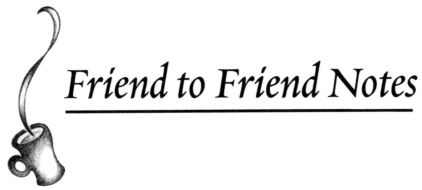

Friend to Friend Notes

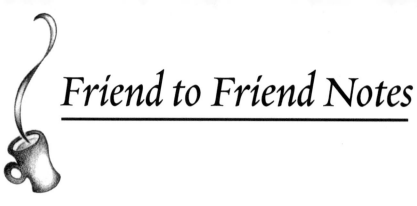

Friend to Friend Notes

Friend to Friend Notes

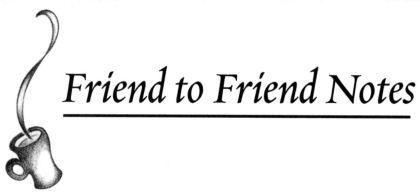

Friend to Friend Notes

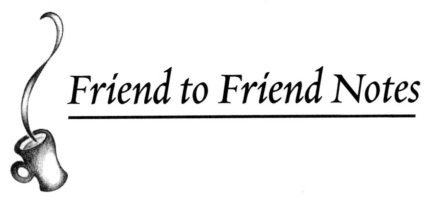

Friend to Friend Notes

Also by Edna Ellison

coauthored with Tricia Scribner

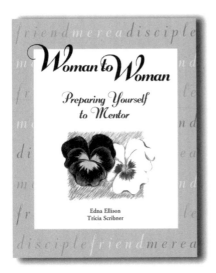

Christian mentors are not "superwomen." They are real people who care enough about others to invest themselves in relationships. This book offers practical advice to help you explore your interest in mentoring by taking you step by step through the process. *Woman to Woman* has a workbook format with a scriptural outline.

N994119 • $12.99 • 1-56309-364-2

An overwhelming number of today's Christian women crave the emotional intimacy of having a mentor, but don't know how to begin or nurture a mentoring relationship. Here's practical help. With an interactive approach, *Seeking Wisdom* shows you:

- how to know where to find a mentor
- how to approach a potential mentor
- how much time to invest in the relationship
- how to relate to mentors of different age groups

N014125 • $12.99 • 1-56309-740-0

Available in Christian bookstores everywhere.

New Hope
Publishers

Equipping You to Share the Hope of Christ